Number 123
Fall 2009

New Directions for Evaluation

Sandra Mathison
Editor-in-Chief

Evaluation Policy and Evaluation Practice

William M. K. Trochim
Melvin M. Mark
Leslie J. Cooksy
Editors

EVALUATION POLICY AND EVALUATION PRACTICE
William M. K. Trochim, Melvin M. Mark, Leslie J. Cooksy (eds.)
New Directions for Evaluation, no. 123
Sandra Mathison, Editor-in-Chief

Microfilm copies of issues and articles are available in 16mm and 35mm, as well as microfiche in 105mm, through University Microfilms Inc., 300 North Zeeb Road, Ann Arbor, Michigan 48106-1346.

New Directions for Evaluation is indexed in Cambridge Scientific Abstracts (CSA/CIG), Contents Pages in Education (T & F), Educational Research Abstracts Online (T & F), ERIC Database (Education Resources Information Center), Higher Education Abstracts (Claremont Graduate University), Social Services Abstracts (CSA/CIG), Sociological Abstracts (CSA/CIG), and Worldwide Political Sciences Abstracts (CSA/CIG).

NEW DIRECTIONS FOR EVALUATION (ISSN 1097-6736, electronic ISSN 1534-875X) is part of The Jossey-Bass Education Series and is published quarterly by Wiley Subscription Services, Inc., A Wiley Company, at Jossey-Bass, 989 Market Street, San Francisco, California 94103-1741.

SUBSCRIPTIONS cost $85 for U.S./Canada/Mexico; $109 international. For institutions, agencies, and libraries, $256 U.S.; $296 Canada/Mexico; $330 international. Prices subject to change.

EDITORIAL CORRESPONDENCE should be addressed to the Editor-in-Chief, Sandra Mathison, University of British Columbia, 2125 Main Mall, Vancouver, BC V6T 1Z4, Canada.

www.josseybass.com

Editorial Policy and Procedures

New Directions for Evaluation, a quarterly sourcebook, is an official publication of the American Evaluation Association. The journal publishes empirical, methodological, and theoretical works on all aspects of evaluation. A reflective approach to evaluation is an essential strand to be woven through every issue. The editors encourage issues that have one of three foci: (1) craft issues that present approaches, methods, or techniques that can be applied in evaluation practice, such as the use of templates, case studies, or survey research; (2) professional issues that present topics of import for the field of evaluation, such as utilization of evaluation or locus of evaluation capacity; (3) societal issues that draw out the implications of intellectual, social, or cultural developments for the field of evaluation, such as the women's movement, communitarianism, or multiculturalism. A wide range of substantive domains is appropriate for *New Directions for Evaluation;* however, the domains must be of interest to a large audience within the field of evaluation. We encourage a diversity of perspectives and experiences within each issue, as well as creative bridges between evaluation and other sectors of our collective lives.

The editors do not consider or publish unsolicited single manuscripts. Each issue of the journal is devoted to a single topic, with contributions solicited, organized, reviewed, and edited by a guest editor. Issues may take any of several forms, such as a series of related chapters, a debate, or a long article followed by brief critical commentaries. In all cases, the proposals must follow a specific format, which can be obtained from the editor-in-chief. These proposals are sent to members of the editorial board and to relevant substantive experts for peer review. The process may result in acceptance, a recommendation to revise and resubmit, or rejection. However, the editors are committed to working constructively with potential guest editors to help them develop acceptable proposals.

Sandra Mathison, Editor-in-Chief
University of British Columbia
2125 Main Mall
Vancouver, BC V6T 1Z4
CANADA
e-mail: nde@eval.org

CONTENTS

EDITORS' NOTES   1
William M. K. Trochim, Melvin M. Mark, Leslie J. Cooksy

1. Evaluation Policy: An Introduction and Overview   3
Melvin M. Mark, Leslie J. Cooksy, William M. K. Trochim
This chapter addresses foundational questions in evaluation policy:
What is evaluation policy? How does it influence evaluation practice?
What are the major kinds of evaluation policies that affect the practice
of evaluation? What policies should guide identification and selection of
evaluators and the timing, planning, budgeting and funding, contracting, implementation, methods and approaches, reporting, and use and
dissemination of evaluations? How can evaluators and AEA become
more engaged in shaping effective evaluation policies?

2. Evaluation Policy and Evaluation Practice   13
William M. K. Trochim
Major conceptual and methodological issues in evaluation policy and
practice are discussed in this chapter. It describes a practical model for
development and revision of evaluation policies, presents a generic
framework for a comprehensive set of evaluation policies, and considers critical challenges and opportunities for the future of evaluation policy and its relationship to practice.

3. Golden Is the Sand: Memory and Hope in Evaluation Policy   33
and Evaluation Practice
Lois-ellin Datta
Situating evaluation policy in the context of the past and with an eye to
the future, this chapter raises questions about current evaluation policy discussions, including the extent to which these discussions consider the diversity of the field, the distribution of evaluation resources,
and the role of future evaluators. The chapter concludes with a vision
for how future discourse on evaluation policy can address and build on
these considerations.

4. Integrating Evaluation Units Into the Political Environment   51
of Government: The Role of Evaluation Policy
Eleanor Chelimsky
This chapter focuses on the organizational and structural considerations
that facilitate doing needed studies, keeping them independent and credible, ensuring their usefulness, and getting them disseminated. The
chapter argues that evaluation's failures can be traced directly to our
naïveté about power relationships in government and to the difficulty of
protecting evaluative independence in the face of political pressure.

5. Evaluation Policy in the European Union and Its Institutions 67

Elliot Stern

This chapter explores some of the specific ways in which European and European Union (EU) evaluation has evolved. EU evaluation policy is described, as is the way it supports the spread of evaluation across Europe. New substantive policy instruments, and their implications for the evolution of evaluation policy, are discussed. EU evaluation policy is considered in the context of alternative narratives for the EU itself and in terms of implications for EU member states.

6. Evaluation Policy in the Netherlands 87

Frans L. Leeuw

This chapter describes developments in evaluation policy in the Netherlands and the role of various actors, including the National Audit Office and the Finance Ministry. It examines trends such as the booming evaluation industry discovered in recent years and considers the role of the Dutch Evaluation Society in the development of national evaluation policies. The chapter summarizes what others can learn from the Dutch experience and what the Dutch can learn from their history.

7. Evaluation Policy and Evaluation Practice: Where Do We Go From Here? 103

Leslie J. Cooksy, Melvin M. Mark, William M. K. Trochim

This final chapter synthesizes key themes and issues presented, including the settings and foci of evaluation policy, and it discusses the implications of these themes for the future of evaluation policy and evaluation practice.

INDEX 111

Editors' Notes

Interest in the topic of evaluation policy has been growing over the last several years, spurred at first by policies related to methodology, but broadened since then by a realization that evaluation policy affects all aspects of our practice. In this issue, leaders in the field take various perspectives on evaluation policy, drawing on their expertise and experience. Chapter 1 provides an introduction to evaluation policy, highlights some of the themes brought up in the other chapters, and describes the origin of this *New Directions for Evaluation* issue. In Chapter 2, William M. K. Trochim, who in his role as president of the American Evaluation Association (AEA) selected evaluation policy as the 2008 conference theme, first outlines why evaluation policy is so important and then lays out a taxonomy of evaluation policies and a structure and set of principles to guide our thinking about evaluation policy making. Chapter 3 centers on the role of professional associations in evaluation policy, especially as global perspectives become increasingly important. Specifically, Lois-ellin Datta uses the metaphor of a pushmi-pullyu, an animal with two heads looking in two directions, to draw lessons from the past and reflect on directions for the future of AEA's activities in evaluation policy. In Chapter 4, through a series of examples from her experiences in the Government Accountability Office, Eleanor Chelimsky makes a powerful argument for evaluation policies to protect the independence and credibility of evaluation units in organizations.

Taking the discussion outside the U.S. context, Elliot Stern describes the evaluation policy landscape and institutional setting in the European Union (EU) in Chapter 5, including the policy instruments that have grown out of the EU's dual identities as supranational and decentralized. This is followed by a historical account of the development of evaluation policy in the Netherlands in Chapter 6; Frans L. Leeuw concludes the chapter by examining the current state of Dutch evaluation policy in the framework provided by Trochim in Chapter 2. The last chapter identifies some of the threads in the chapters and suggests next steps.

There are next steps, of course, because this issue covers only a sliver of the topic of evaluation policy. For example, there is no discussion of evaluation policy in political contexts outside the United States or Europe, and the chapters tend to focus on government policies rather than evaluation policies in the nonprofit and for-profit sectors. The intent of the issue is not to be comprehensive so much as to fan the flames of interest in evaluation policy. Ultimately, we hope to increase our understanding of evaluation policy and how we might influence it. As noted in the first chapter, the authors

New Directions for Evaluation, no. 123, Fall 2009 © Wiley Periodicals, Inc. and the American Evaluation Association. Published online in Wiley InterScience (www.interscience.wiley.com) • DOI: 10.1002/ev.301

1

included in the volume offer some hope that the area of evaluation policy is one in which evaluators, individually and collaboratively, can make a difference.

William M. K. Trochim
Melvin M. Mark
Leslie J. Cooksy
Editors

WILLIAM M. K. TROCHIM is professor of policy analysis and management at Cornell University and is the director of evaluation for the Weill Cornell Clinical and Translational Science Center, the director of evaluation for extension and outreach, and the director of the Cornell Office for Research on Evaluation.

MELVIN M. MARK is professor and head of psychology at the Pennsylvania State University. He has served as president of the American Evaluation Association and as editor of the American Journal of Evaluation (now editor emeritus).

LESLIE J. COOKSY, incoming president of the American Evaluation Association, is an associate professor at the University of Delaware, where she directs a graduate program in evaluation.

NEW DIRECTIONS FOR EVALUATION • DOI: 10.1002/ev

Mark, M. M., Cooksy, L. J., & Trochim, W.M.K. (2009). Evaluation policy: An introduction and overview. In W.M.K. Trochim, M. M. Mark, & L. J. Cooksy (Eds.), *Evaluation policy and evaluation practice. New Directions for Evaluation, 123*, 3–11.

1

Evaluation Policy: An Introduction and Overview

Melvin M. Mark, Leslie J. Cooksy, William M. K. Trochim

Abstract

Evaluation policy is of considerable importance, especially in relation to the limited amount of attention it receives as a general topic in the mainstream evaluation literature. Evaluation policies matter for several reasons, among them that they can profoundly affect evaluation practice, they underlie many recent and current controversies about evaluation, and they may be a lever for change that can have far-reaching effects for practice. This chapter gives an overview of several issues regarding evaluation policy, including defining it, identifying possible facets of evaluation policy, describing how it is established, and outlining the potentially greater role for evaluators in shaping the evaluation policies that influence evaluation practice. © Wiley Periodicals, Inc.

This issue of *New Directions for Evaluation* is based on several related beliefs about evaluation policy. First, evaluation policy is a critical concern for evaluation practice, in part because it shapes evaluation practice, thereby both enabling and constraining the potential contribution evaluation can make. For example, if the legislation that establishes a pilot program specifies a particular type of summative evaluation and no other evaluation activities, the pilot program may not benefit from the more developmental

and formative functions of evaluation. At the extreme, evaluation policy may not only enable some forms of contribution and constrain others; bad evaluation policy can have serious negative consequences. For example, consider two areas of work outside the traditional emphasis of most American Evaluation Association (AEA) evaluators. Critics have argued essentially that flawed evaluation policies at the Food and Drug Administration underlay the controversy over Vioxx a few years ago (U.S. Senate, 2004). In the case of auditing, a function related to evaluation, an argument can similarly be made that bad audit policy was at the root of Arthur Andersen's contribution to the rise and fall of Enron (McLean & Elkind, 2003).

A second underlying belief is that evaluation policy deserves more explicit attention in the formal literature and informal dialogue about evaluation. For example, students taking training in evaluation can complete their coursework with little focus if any on evaluation policy. To be fair, in one sense attention to evaluation policy is ubiquitous, in that most writing about evaluation at least implicitly suggests preferences for evaluation policy. At the same time, there is a paucity of literature explicitly addressing the topic of evaluation policy, broadly construed—its origins, how it is developed, the evidence base for evaluation policies, examples of coherent evaluation policies in use, the consequences of having one evaluation policy rather than another, and so on. As another example of the desirability of expanding explicit attention to evaluation policy, it would be interesting to see the preferences of evaluators of various theoretical persuasions. We might speculate, for instance, that certain theorists would highlight methods in their preferred evaluation policies, while others would place more emphasis for policies guiding stakeholder involvement (cf. Alkin, 2004). To take yet another example, more explicit attention to evaluation policy could enrich and improve some of the discourse in which evaluators engage. In particular, evaluators may fail to notice that debate seeming to be about methods is actually better understood as debate about evaluation policies. In the next chapter, for example, Trochim posits that contemporary debate about randomized trials may involve a failure of evaluation policy development, with high-level policy developers creating excessively specific policies that fail to delegate enough authority for decision making at lower levels in the governance hierarchy.

A third belief is that greater involvement of evaluators in development of evaluation policy, if carried out well, could open the door to significant improvements in future evaluation practice. For example, by informing policy makers about what would constitute good evaluation policy, evaluators and their associations might help in constructing evaluation policies that will facilitate evaluations with greater value. We return to this topic later.

Before addressing these and other points, however, we need to clarify what evaluation policy is and is not, especially because confusion can easily arise. By *evaluation policy* we mean policies such as (but not only) high-level rules embedded in legislation that are used to guide the practice of evaluation. Thus, when Congress passes a bill to carry out a trial of a program called Early Head Start and in the legislation it mandates a randomized trial, evaluation policy has been set. More generally, in Chapter 2 of this issue Trochim defines evaluation policy as "any rule or principle that a group or organization uses to guide its decisions and actions when doing evaluation." In contrast, most of the time when the terms *evaluation* and *policy* are used in the same sentence, the focus is on how evaluation findings (and sometimes process) affect policy in a given area. For example, much has been made of the effects of the Perry Preschool evaluation and other related work on the movement for universal pre-K in the United States (e.g., Schweinhart et al., 2005). In cases such as this, the emphasis is *not* on what we are calling evaluation policy. Rather, the focus in the Perry Preschool case and related ones is on how specific evaluations may influence policy in areas such as early childhood education. In contrast, evaluation policy, as we are using the term, refers to rules or principles that help set the content, characteristics, and context of *evaluation itself*.

The Definition and Scope of Evaluation Policy

Having differentiated "evaluation policy" from "evaluation and its influence on substantive policy," we need to quickly acknowledge that further attention is called for in defining evaluation policy.

Formal and Informal Policy. One important definitional issue involves whether evaluation policy includes implicit and informal guidance about evaluation, as well as explicit and formal guidance. On the one hand, most observers are likely to agree that evaluation policy has been set when a high level of governance (e.g., Congress, a state department of education, the board of directors of a foundation) formally and explicitly specifies a broad rule that is intended to govern one or more aspects of evaluation. Examples include Great Society legislation that mandated evaluation of new programs and the Department of Health and Human Services "set-asides" that create a pool of funding for evaluation (Shadish, Cook, & Leviton, 1991), the more recent Department of Education priority that specifies a preference for randomized trials for selected funding streams (Donaldson, Christie, & Mark, 2009), the mandate by which monitoring and evaluation findings are reported to citizens including via the Internet in South Africa (National Treasury, 2007), the multifaceted statement of evaluation policy for international development recently put forward by the United Kingdom department working in this area (Department for International Development, 2009), and some foundations' decision that the evaluation unit will report directly to the foundation president.

In defining evaluation policy, however, an argument exists for a broader scope that would include more informally held rules, as well as the more formally developed policies. Trochim contends in the next chapter that informal, implicit rules should be included under the umbrella of evaluation

NEW DIRECTIONS FOR EVALUATION • DOI: 10.1002/ev

policy. Consider, for example, a foundation or state agency where everyone knows that all evaluations should begin with development of a logic model, but no one can point to a written dictate or say when and how this informal rule came to be. Trochim considers these informal rules to be evaluation policies, even if no one can lay out the "policy making" that led to their existence. An analogy to substantive policy making supports this inclusion of more informal, perhaps even emergent, rules as policy. In the area of foreign policy, an old adage states that policy is "made on the wires," that is, developed in real time in the cables wired back and forth between an embassy and State Department staffers.

Unlike Trochim, several of the other authors in this issue appear to focus on more explicit evaluation policies. This does not, however, mean that the authors would exclude more implicit and informal policies from the realm of evaluation policy. In any event, we support a broader and more inclusive definition of evaluation policy. In addition, the informal-formal distinction may lead to interesting hypotheses, regardless of how expansive a definition one endorses. In particular, an argument can be made that benefits will result when informal evaluation policies are converted to more explicit ones, *if* the process of developing more informed policies is informed, fair, and reflective of the multiple purposes of evaluation. By contrast, poorly developed, explicit, formal evaluation policies may create more problems than would occur in the presence of informal policies only.

Facets of Evaluation Policy. What aspects of evaluation should and do evaluation policies cover? When evaluators are asked to think about evaluation policy, many of them may tend to think first of policies that guide the methods for carrying out an evaluation. Contemporary debates about the place of randomized controlled trials (RCTs) reflect one example in which the focus of evaluation policy is on methods. However, evaluation policy can specify a range of characteristics related to evaluation. What gets evaluated—all programs, certain programs, clusters of related programs rather than individual programs? Which evaluation methods are to be used (and under what conditions)? What is the process by which contingent, situationally responsive method choices are to be made? How are evaluations funded, contracted, overseen? How are evaluators to be selected? Is there some credential that evaluators should have? What are the structural relations surrounding evaluation (e.g., is there an independent evaluation shop in an agency)? How are various stakeholders to be involved, and when? What practices are to be undertaken for reporting, dissemination, and facilitation of use?

Trochim, in Chapter 2, offers an eight-wedge "evaluation policy wheel" intended to capture the various facets that comprehensive evaluation policy should cover. In Chapter 3, Datta offers a related set of questions that evaluation policy could address. A clear message is that evaluation policy can, and in the ideal should, address a number of considerations, ranging from management to method to participation. Of course, in practice actual

NEW DIRECTIONS FOR EVALUATION • DOI: 10.1002/ev

evaluation policies will often be incomplete, addressing some but not all of the potential facets.

How Evaluation Policy Is Set

Perhaps not surprisingly, there is not a single, generalizable answer to the question of how evaluation policy is set. Evaluation policy setting will likely vary: across executive and legislative branches; across federal, state, and local governments; across government, foundation, NGO, and private organizations; across the United States and other countries; across formal and informal policies; and across the specifics of one situation versus another. In addition, just as various theoretical approaches that emphasize different actors and process have been proposed to explain the development of substantive policy (e.g., Bennett & Howlett, 1992), alternative frameworks could be employed to account for creation and revision of evaluation policy. Drawing on these alternative frameworks as well as experience, we offer several suggestions about the development of evaluation policy:

- There are multiple ways for evaluation policy to be set, at different times and places.
- Evaluation policy is sometimes used as a lever to accomplish other ends (e.g., delaying general action by mandating evaluation of a policy program).
- At times evaluation policy is an afterthought, tacked on late to substantive policy.
- Without the involvement of evaluators, those who set evaluation policy may not appreciate the multiple contributions that evaluation can bring.
- Often there will be windows of opportunity (e.g., as legislation is being developed) when it is more feasible to influence evaluation policy.
- In many instances, opportunities may exist to influence some facets of evaluation policy (e.g., institutional arrangements of the sort Chelimsky focuses on in this issue) but not all facets of a comprehensive policy.
- Regardless of the process by which it is developed, evaluation policy affects evaluation practice.
- Efforts by evaluators to contribute to the development of evaluation policy ideally will be carried out in ways that also enhance democratic values and good governance.

The Potential Role of Evaluators in Establishing Evaluation Policy

Evaluators can play a role in setting and revising evaluation capacity, acting as individuals, in various networks, and collectively through their professional associations. Well-positioned evaluators, individually and in networks, have been instrumental in developing, maintaining (sometimes in the face of opposition), and improving evaluation policies in the organizations in which they work. Examples are available in this issue of *NDE*, especially in the contributions by Chelimsky and Leeuw, although the evaluator's contribution is not always explicitly highlighted. Although the action of individuals and informal networks can be powerful, we focus here on professional association involvement, in part because this has been an area with recent activity and with promising potential for the future.

American Evaluation Association (AEA) Activities

In October 2007, AEA announced formation of the association's Evaluation Policy Task Force (EPTF). Authorized initially for two years, the goal of the EPTF is "to assist AEA in developing an ongoing capability to influence evaluation policies that are critically important to the practice of evaluation" (American Evaluation Association, 2007). Eight members were appointed to the EPTF (Eleanor Chelimsky, Leslie Cooksy, Katherine Dawes, Patrick Grasso, Susan Kistler, Mel Mark, Stephanie Shipman, and William Trochim as chair). George Grob, president of the Center for Public Program Evaluation, was contracted to serve as a consultant. A strategic decision was made to focus the initial EPTF on evaluation policies in the U.S. federal government.

In its relatively short existence, the EPFT has been engaged in notable activities. Of particular interest is its involvement with the U.S. Office of Management and Budget (OMB). A key early step was a meeting of the EPTF chair and consultant with Robert Shea, then the associate director of OMB for administration and government performance, and a key person in the agency's design and use of the Program Assessment Rating Tool (PART), a key evaluative mechanism in recent years. Following that meeting, Shea invited detailed comments from the EPTF on a document titled "What Constitutes Strong Evidence of a Program's Effectiveness?" which had been cited approvingly in OMB's PART guidance. The EPTF comments were well received. More recently, the EPTF prepared an "Evaluation Roadmap for a More Effective Government," which was transmitted to Peter Orszag, the new director of OMB in the Obama administration. The EPTF and its consultant have also been involved in several other activities aimed at contributing to federal policy in specific areas and in building relationships and trust to facilitate future work.

As this volume goes to press, the story of the EPTF continues to evolve. For example, it has recently sent recommendations (on request) to both House and Senate committees responsible for health care reform. In its ongoing work, the EPTF continues to seek to influence evaluation policies at the U.S. federal level. As this early experience suggests, there appears to be reason for at least guarded optimism that collective action by evaluators can contribute to more thoughtful consideration of evaluation policy by those who can set it. Moreover, this may prove to be a case in which practice informs theory in the sense that the activities of the EPTF, and of other similar efforts, help advance understanding of evaluation policy setting.

One of the key challenges in an association's efforts to affect policies is ensuring that the efforts represent the interest of members, without turning the endeavor into pablum and platitudes. In the case of AEA's EPTF, several steps were taken to facilitate involvement of AEA members, including a special page on the organization's website (http://www.eval.org/EPTF.asp), sessions on the initiative at the 2007 and 2008 annual conferences, an electronic discussion listserv, and periodic announcements in the AEA newsletter. Overall, the feedback received from members was quite encouraging of the task force's activities. In addition to contact with members, the EPTF has reported periodically to the AEA board. The EPTF has also included at least two members who are on the board as president, president-elect, or past-president. This has helped ensure the EPFT did not drift from the intentions of the association's elected leadership. Nevertheless, one of the long-term challenges of an evaluation policy initiative involves managing the tension among (1) offering a timely response when a window of opportunity appears; (2) representing well the values and interests of the association, the broader field, and those who may benefit from evaluation; and (3) facilitating development of better evaluation policy while being neither too general to be useful nor too specific to be respectful of the diversity within evaluation practice.

A Note Regarding Origins

This issue of *NDE* has its direct and immediate origins in the 2008 AEA annual conference. Bill Trochim, the 2008 president, selected the topic of evaluation policy for the conference theme. The chapters in this issue, with the exception of the opening and closing ones, were all based on the plenary addresses and expert lectures presented in the conference's Presidential Strand (which was co-chaired by Leslie Cooksy and Mel Mark). There is, however, a longer and more circuitous set of connections that helped lead to the current issue. Evaluation policy, though often discussed in a broader context, has been of considerable interest to AEA boards and presidents for some time. For example, before, during, and after Mark's term as president in 2006, there was frequent conversation about how AEA should "be at the table" when important decisions were being made by federal agencies and other groups about how evaluation should be done. These conversations translated into such actions as the AEA EPTF and the Public Forums that have become a regular feature of the AEA annual conference. The forums are organized by the Public Affairs Committee (PAC), starting with the first in 2006, which was organized by then-PAC chair Bill Trochim, and addressed PART from multiple perspectives. Between involvement in EPTF and PAC (which Cooksy chaired in 2008), Trochim, Cooksy, and Mark have had the opportunity to learn about evaluation policy from such people as

George Grob, EPTF consultant; the other EPTF members; the PAC members; and the participants in the PAC forums, among others.

Several interrelated points arise from this brief and seemingly solipsistic history. First, interest in the topic of evaluation policy has a longer and broader history than that of one year's conference theme. Indeed, we would like to think it is a topic whose time has come. Second, the issue editors owe a debt of gratitude to many colleagues not listed here, among them several past presidents of AEA as well as fellow members of AEA's board, PAC, and EPTF. Thanks to those and others! Third, the editors of this issue wish to express their gratitude for the privilege of being in positions that allow them to try to move things ahead in terms of evaluators' thinking about and acting on evaluation policy. Finally, this brief history, as well as the stories told in several of the chapters in this issue (especially those by Leeuw, Chelimsky, and Stern), offer some hope that the area of evaluation policy is one in which evaluators, individually and collaboratively, can at times make a difference.

Caveats and Conclusions

We hasten to add several caveats about the presentation of evaluation policy. First, although evaluation policy is a topic that applies at various levels of government, and to nongovernmental organizations and various sectors, the chapters in this issue of *NDE* focus on national (U.S. federal) and to some extent supranational (e.g., EEU) units. This is not to imply that evaluation policy is more important, or easier (or harder), at these levels than at others. Rather, given the potentially wide range of territory that could be covered, we chose to focus our efforts (similar consideration has led the EPTF to focus on U.S. federal evaluation policy). Expanding on this focus is one potentially valuable direction for future work on evaluation policy. This may be especially important because organizations may vary tremendously in their capacity and willingness to develop evaluation policies, at least of the more formal and explicit variety. In addition, the best processes for influencing evaluation policy may prove to differ across type of organization.

Second, we have likewise focused primarily on program evaluation (although some chapters veer into policy evaluation and audit). Again, this choice should not be taken as implying that evaluation policies apply to program evaluation and not to other types of evaluation (or to related endeavors). Our sense is that much of what is said here in the context of program evaluation will generalize to other related endeavors, and we encourage exploration or refutation of this suggestion.

A third caveat arises from an earlier observation that there has been a paucity of past work done explicitly on the topic of evaluation policy. In part as a consequence, we do not see the work captured in this issue as an enduring statement. Rather, we hope to stimulate additional work, both conceptual and empirical, that will expand and adjust our current understanding of evaluation policy.

NEW DIRECTIONS FOR EVALUATION • DOI: 10.1002/ev

A fourth caveat applies to taking action intended to help shape development of better evaluation policy. It would be naïve to expect that most organizations will, overnight, acquire the capacity and motivation to develop sound and comprehensive evaluation policies. Nevertheless, there is reason for optimism that thoughtful, concerted effort on the part of evaluators can contribute to worthwhile improvement in the evaluation policies that affect our work and the contributions it can make.

References

Alkin, M. (Ed.). (2004). *Evaluation roots: Tracing theorists' views and influences*. Thousand Oaks, CA: Sage.

American Evaluation Association. (2007, October 17). *EPTF announcement letter*. Retrieved April 2, 2009, from http://www.eval.org/EPTF.asp

Bennett, C. J., & Howlett, M. (1992). The lessons of learning: Reconciling theories of policy learning and policy change. *Policy Sciences, 25*, 275–294.

Department for International Development. (2009, June). *Building the evidence to reduce poverty: The UK's policy on evaluation for international development*. Retrieved July 7, 2009, from http://www.eval.org/EPTF.asp

Donaldson, S., Christie, T. C., & Mark, M. M. (2009). *What counts as credible evidence in applied research and evaluation practice?* Thousand Oaks, CA: Sage.

McLean, B., & Elkind, P. (2003). *Smartest guys in the room: The amazing rise and scandalous fall of Enron*. New York: Penguin.

National Treasury. (2007). *Framework for managing programme performance information*. Pretoria: National Treasury, Republic of South Africa. Retrieved July 8, 2009, from http://www.thepresidency.gov.za/main.asp?include=learning/reference/framework/index.html

Schweinhart, L. J., Montie, J., Xiang, Z., Barnett, W. S., Belfield, C. R., & Nores, M. (2005). Lifetime effects: The HighScope Perry Preschool study through age 40. *Monographs of the HighScope Educational Research Foundation, 14*.

Shadish, W. R., Cook, T. D., & Leviton, L. C. (1991). *Foundations of program evaluation: Theories of practice*. Thousand Oaks, CA: Sage.

U.S. Senate (2004, Nov. 18). FDA, Merck and Vioxx: *Putting patient safety first?* Retrieved January 13, 2005, from http://finance.senate. gov/sitepages/hearing111804.htm

MELVIN M. MARK is professor and head of psychology at the Pennsylvania State University. He has served as president of the American Evaluation Association and as editor of the American Journal of Evaluation *(now editor emeritus).*

LESLIE J. COOKSY, incoming president of the American Evaluation Association, is an associate professor at the University of Delaware, where she directs a graduate program in evaluation.

WILLIAM M. K. TROCHIM is professor of policy analysis and management at Cornell University and is the director of evaluation for the Weill Cornell Clinical and Translational Science Center, the director of evaluation for extension and outreach, and the director of the Cornell Office for Research on Evaluation.

Trochim, W.M.K. (2009). Evaluation policy and evaluation practice. In W.M.K. Trochim, M. M. Mark, & L. J. Cooksy (Eds.), *Evaluation policy and evaluation practice. New Directions for Evaluation, 123,* 13–32.

2

Evaluation Policy and Evaluation Practice

William M. K. Trochim

Abstract

The author develops the basic idea of evaluation policy, describes a practical model for development and revision of evaluation policies (including a taxonomy, structure, and set of principles), and suggests critical challenges and opportunities for the future of evaluation policy. An evaluation policy is any rule or principle that a group or organization uses to guide its decisions and actions when doing evaluation. Every entity that engages in evaluation, including government agencies, private businesses, and nonprofit organizations, has evaluation policies. Sometimes they are explicit and written; more often they are implicit and ad hoc principles or norms that have simply evolved over time.

This work was supported in part by grants from the National Science Foundation (A Phase II Trial of the Systems Evaluation Protocol for Assessing and Improving STEM Education Evaluation. DRL. NSF Grant 0814364; Evaluation Systems and Systems Evaluation: Building Capacity and Tools for Enhancing STEM Education Evaluation. HER/REC/EREC. NSF Grant 0535492) and the National Institutes of Health (NIH/ NCRR. Institutional Clinical and Translational Science Award, U54. NIH Grant 1 UL1 RR024996-01). The author wishes to thank Margaret Johnson for her editorial contributions and to recognize the incredible efforts of Mel Mark and Leslie Cooksy through their support, encouragement, and detailed input both in preparation of the Presidential Strand on "Evaluation Policy and Evaluation Practice" at the 2008 Annual Conference of the American Evaluation Association and for their assistance in preparation of this manuscript.

Evaluation policies profoundly affect the day-to-day work of all evaluators and ultimately the quality of the programs they evaluate. Many recent and current controversies or conflicts in the field of evaluation can be viewed, at least in part, as a struggle around evaluation policy. Because evaluation policies typically apply across multiple evaluations, influencing policies directly may have systemic and far-reaching effects for practice. Evaluation practice must play a critical role in informing and shaping the development of evaluation policies. © Wiley Periodicals, Inc.

E valuation needs a fresh look at the idea of evaluation policy and its intimate, dynamic connection with evaluation practice. On the one hand, evaluation policy has always been a topic of concern in the field. One can read almost any classic evaluation text or article and cull from it some relevant implications for evaluation policies, ranging from choice of method to involvement of relevant stakeholders to the importance of addressing ethical and regulatory issues, and so on. On the other hand, most of the potential implications for evaluation policies are necessarily couched in the conditional and qualifying language of theory. One searches the evaluation literature in vain for context-specific sets of candidate policies, for guidelines on expressing such policies, and for ways of managing and evaluating them to achieve better policies over time.

The underlying and self-consciously provocative thesis of this chapter is that developing well-informed evaluation policies that can guide evaluation practice may be the most important issue currently facing our field. It's more important than getting our methods right, or concerns about validity. It's more important than the ethics of evaluation. It's more important than making evaluation participatory, or using it for empowerment. Why? Because evaluation policy encompasses all of those things and more. It touches virtually everything we think about or do in evaluation.

This chapter aims to accomplish several things. First is the obvious need to attempt a definition of evaluation policy, describe its relationship with practice, and in general identify some of the major conceptual issues involved. Second, a methodology will be offered that can be used for managing evaluation policies in contexts ranging from large and complex systems such as the federal government to local evaluations conducted in small organizations or groups. This methodological model includes a taxonomy of evaluation policy types, a structure for managing policy complexity, and a set of principles that can guide policy development. Some fragmentary and suggestive initial examples of how evaluation policies operate and are organized will be offered. Finally, some of the challenges that we face in evolving the idea of evaluation policy will be discussed and potential opportunities considered. In the end, all roads in this chapter lead back to the primary thesis: *evaluators need to get serious about evaluation policy and its relationship to practice.*

NEW DIRECTIONS FOR EVALUATION • DOI: 10.1002/ev

Evaluation Policy: Definitional and Conceptual Issues

A major housekeeping issue we have to address before we can get into the heart of this discussion is the confusion between evaluation policy and the traditional idea of policy. When most people think about the term *policy* they probably think first about big policy, major national policy, well-known policies that are familiar to us all. For instance, they might think about John Kennedy in 1961 saying, "This nation should commit itself to achieving the goal, before this decade is out, of landing a man on the moon and returning him safely to earth." This certainly qualifies as a major policy statement, one that successfully shaped the efforts of a generation. The statement had some of the key characteristics one might expect in any high-level general policy. It had a definable outcome in mind. It had a clear time-frame. As is typical of policies, it is a general statement that does not describe how it will be achieved operationally; Kennedy didn't talk about payloads, lunar landers, or astronauts drinking Tang. In fact, they probably didn't even have Tang at that point. Kennedy's statement can be considered a broad or high-level *substantive* policy.

Here's another example, more recent, from then-candidate Barack Obama, who in August 2008 said, "If I am president, I will immediately direct the full resources of the federal government and the full energy of the private sector to a single, overarching goal: in ten years, we will eliminate the need for oil from the entire Middle East and Venezuela." Now, that was not at the time a policy because he was not yet president, but should he carry the statement into his administration it will become a policy, a very high-level substantive policy. Notice that he doesn't talk about the details of how he is going to implement that policy. The policy simply circumscribes the direction that more detailed policy and practice would take.

So let's begin with a distinction between what will be termed here "substantive policy" and "evaluation policy," as depicted in Figure 2.1. It is tempting to use the term *public policy* rather than substantive policy, because the former is more familiar in evaluation circles, but there are policies other than just "public" ones, and the intent here is to distinguish evaluation policy from *any* kind of substantive policy, public or otherwise. When most people think of substantive policy they typically have in mind the types of statements articulated by Kennedy and Obama. Usually policies of that sort get translated into operational objects and practices such as lunar landers, Tang for astronauts, special new technologies for fuel efficiency, training and simulation programs, and so on. That is, we might call the stuff that policies are translated into its programs or practices. There is an often complex translation that occurs in operationalizing substantive policies into practices: high-level policies are typically translated into more specific subpolicies on the way to their manifestation in practice.

There is a dynamic throughout the life of a policy, and the programs or activities associated with it. Evaluation plays a critical role in providing

Figure 2.1. The Relationship Between Substantive and Evaluation Policy

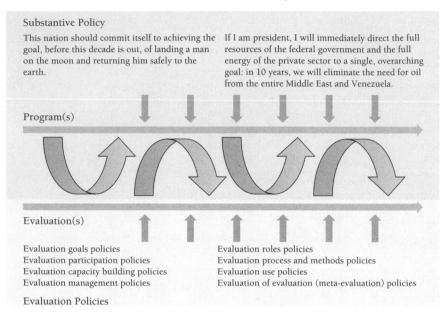

Substantive Policy

This nation should commit itself to achieving the goal, before this decade is out, of landing a man on the moon and returning him safely to the earth.

If I am president, I will immediately direct the full resources of the federal government and the full energy of the private sector to a single, overarching goal: in 10 years, we will eliminate the need for oil from the entire Middle East and Venezuela.

Program(s)

Evaluation(s)

Evaluation goals policies
Evaluation participation policies
Evaluation capacity building policies
Evaluation management policies

Evaluation roles policies
Evaluation process and methods policies
Evaluation use policies
Evaluation of evaluation (meta-evaluation) policies

Evaluation Policies

essential feedback about what's happening in the programs or practices or technologies associated with policies. Evaluation policies guide how evaluation happens, as depicted at the bottom of Figure 2.1 (which also foreshadows the categories of policies that we will include in our taxonomy). That is, evaluation policies can shape evaluation practice. In turn, evaluation serves programs and activities and, through them, the substantive policies that guide them. But there is a clear distinction between evaluation policies and the substantive policies they serve. With this important distinction in place, the remainder of this chapter sets aside the issue of broad substantive policy and concentrates on the topic of evaluation policy and its relationship to evaluation practice.

Definition of Evaluation Policy. What is evaluation policy? Here's a potential simple formal definition: *An evaluation policy is any rule or principle that a group or organization uses to guide its decisions and actions when doing evaluation.*

Every group and organization that engages in evaluation—including government agencies, private businesses, and nonprofit organizations—has evaluation policies. Sometimes they are written and explicit; at other times they are unwritten and implicit, ad hoc principles or norms that have simply evolved over time. The contention here is that all evaluations are *already* guided by policy, whether the protagonists involved in them recognize or acknowledge it or not. The problem is that most of the policies that guide evaluations are unwritten. You would have a hard time pointing to them; they are not transparent either to those within the organization or to those outside. In the absence of written evaluation policies, organizations often seem to make up policies as they go along—too often without consulting others on what they have done or informing themselves about evaluation best practices.

One of the key definitional questions about policy has to do with how we distinguish it from other things that are potentially confused with it. For instance, how do we tell the difference between a policy and a guideline, a policy and a standard, or a policy and a theory? The argument here is that standards, guidelines, and theories become policies only if and when they are consciously adopted to guide decisions or actions about evaluation and when the organization institutes consequences for encouraging or enforcing them. If we have an evaluation theory or approach, such as utilization-focused evaluation (Patton, 2008), empowerment evaluation (Fetterman, Kaftarian, & Wandersman, 1996), theory-driven evaluation (Chen & Rossi, 1990), or any other of the worthy forms of evaluation, those are simply what they are: theories or approaches. They become evaluation policy when an organization decides it is going to use this approach or adopt this theory in doing evaluations; failing to do so will have consequences.

These two characteristics of policy—consciousness and consequence—are not always consistent within an organization. For instance, it may be the case that some people, such as upper management, hold evaluation policy expectations and attempt to incentivize or enforce their use while at the same time others in their organization have their own expectations, or are unaware of their views, or are uninfluenced by their efforts at enforcing them. This is one of the major justifications for encouraging that evaluation policies be written and communicated.

Why Is Evaluation Policy Important? Why should we care about written evaluation policies and how they are developed? First, evaluation policy is valuable for its signaling role. An evaluation policy can be thought of as a type of communication mechanism. It constitutes a signal to the entire organization and its stakeholders, communicating what evaluations should be done, what resources expended, who is responsible, how they should be accomplished, and so on. It can be an efficient way to communicate and encourage consistency in evaluation implementation.

Second, evaluation policies help make evaluation a more transparent and democratic endeavor. They constitute a public stance that an organization takes regarding evaluation. Because they are public, written policies, they can be known by everyone in the organization and thus criticized and challenged. Participation and dialogue can occur about which policies make the most sense under which circumstances.

Third, evaluation policy is also a mechanism for broader learning about evaluation. Preskill (2007) emphasized the value of viewing evaluation as a type of learning. Evaluation policy could be one of the key mechanisms for such learning. Why? Because if we write evaluation policies down, we can archive them. We can share them. We can look at which of them seem to work better in which situations. That is, there can be some cumulative knowledge about what kinds of policies appear to work under various circumstances. We can also use evaluation policy to learn about the connection between evaluation theory and practice. Systematic reviews of evaluation implementation across organizations and settings can compare evaluation policies with respect to feasibility, effectiveness, efficiency, and other characteristics.

Fourth, evaluation policy is potentially an efficient mechanism for changing practice. For instance, if you want to change an evaluation practice in a large organization (e.g., the government), you typically have to go to each specific context and make the change locally. But if evaluation policies affect evaluation practice, the easier and more efficient way would be to change the overall policy once and have that change cascade to all relevant practice subcontexts.

Finally, evaluation policy is important because many of the controversies in evaluation today are essentially about such policy. This is apparent in the debates about the evaluation requirements in the Program Assessment Rating Tool (PART) system of the U.S. Office of Management and Budget (AEA Evaluation Policy Task Force, 2008), where the randomized controlled trial is presented in policy guidance as a preferred methodology for effectiveness evaluation in all programs in the federal government. We encountered similar issues in this association several years ago around regulations—essentially evaluation policies—that the Department of Education was proposing with respect to randomized experiments (Julnes & Rog, 2007; U.S. Department of Education, 2003). Controversies of this kind are fundamentally issues about what evaluation policy should be. There is no ignoring the issue of evaluation policy; it keeps coming back to us.

Who Controls Evaluation Policy? There are several fundamental issues related to power and participation that are central to the evaluation policy development process. Certainly, one of the major questions is who should be involved in formulating policies. The short answer is that evaluation policies will generally be best when there is broad and open involvement in policy development. Participatory approaches help ensure both that important issues don't get overlooked and that there is clearer communication and buy-in about evaluation.

Following closely on the question of who participates is *how* they can be involved most effectively. The field of evaluation has considerable shared experience with encouraging and facilitating participatory collaborative methods (Cousins & Whitmore, 1998; King, 1998), and we can effectively leverage this experience not just for evaluation itself but also in developing evaluation policy.

Questions of power and control are absolutely central to the discussion of evaluation policy. People in a position of power often have primary control over policy making. But it is not clear that policies developed centrally will be appropriate or effective across an organization. Collaboration of stakeholders from throughout the organization will almost surely help encourage development of policies that are more appropriate and feasible.

Finally, no consideration of power and control in evaluation policy would be complete without raising issues related to fears and anxieties about evaluation generally and how they affect formulation of evaluation policy specifically. For instance, we know that many people are concerned about evaluation because they fear, often legitimately, that it may threaten their interests, harm their favorite programs, lead to decisions they don't like, take too much time or too many resources, and so on. Such fears and anxieties inevitably will and should play out in the evaluation policy development process. People will want to be assured that evaluation policies are fair and ethical, work for their perceived interests, and do not impose burdens from their point of view. To the extent that they can control the policy-making process, people will certainly attempt to do so. Evaluation policy development needs to be able to balance the interests of many stakeholders.

This discussion of power and participation does not begin to do justice to the complexities and challenges that must be addressed. We will need good evaluation work about the evaluation policy-making process in order to begin to understand how these issues unfold and what their implications might be. While we await the evolution of such work, and encourage its undertaking, we turn our attention from the broad definitional and conceptual issues to ones that are more methodological in nature.

An Evaluation Policy Methodology

If we are to have effective evaluation policies, we will need to develop methods for creating, archiving, evaluating, and revising them. This section attempts to move us along methodologically by offering an evaluation policy model that includes a taxonomy of evaluation policy types, a structure that depicts the interrelationships between policies and practices, and a set of principles that can be used in developing and managing policies.

Several caveats are in order before venturing onto this ground. First, the methodological framework offered here is only an initial, suggestive one. It has not itself been evaluated, although it is hoped that if it appears promising it will be subjected to extensive testing in practice. Second, the examples that are given here are for the most part created for purposes of this explication. There is a paucity of good evaluation policy examples and relatively few that were identified for this work. Readers should keep this in mind when interpreting these examples and should not use them as models or exemplars of policies recommended for real-world contexts.

Evaluation Policy Model: A Taxonomy. Evaluations are complex endeavors that involve many variations, dimensions, and activities. Commensurately, there will need to be many types of evaluation policies in order to guide this complex endeavor well. Currently we do not have a clear taxonomy of the types of evaluation policies that might make up a comprehensive set of policies. Here is a tentative taxonomy, a list of evaluation policy categories within which we might wish to develop specific policies:

A Draft Taxonomy of Evaluation Policies

- Evaluation goals policies
- Evaluation participation policies
- Evaluation capacity building policies
- Evaluation management policies
- Evaluation roles policies
- Evaluation process and methods policies
- Evaluation use policies
- Evaluation of evaluation (meta-evaluation) policies

It would be preferable to develop a classification system for evaluation policies empirically. For example, one might use an evaluation method such as concept mapping (Kane & Trochim, 2006; Trochim, 1989; Trochim & Kane, 2005) to identify empirically what evaluators think the categories of policy might best be. Such efforts are currently under way, but until the results are in we can only anticipate what they might yield with intuitively based a priori categorizations such as those in the list. There is no single accepted form for expressing evaluation policies. So we are essentially free to experiment with different forms as this field evolves. To illustrate how such policies might look, the examples offered in the taxonomy are expressed in a somewhat formalistic policy language of the type that you might see in standard organizational policy and procedures manuals. Generally, evaluation policies should be relatively short and concise statements, although they may need to be supplemented with notes, definitions, and other explanatory text.

The taxonomy begins with policies that describe the *goals* of evaluation in the organization or context. For example, a general goal policy might be "The primary goals of evaluation in our organization are to learn about and improve programs and to ensure accountability to our stakeholders." One can imagine further subpolicies for each of the two goals in the broad policy. For example, you might describe the program improvement goal further with "Evaluation for program improvement should address both the process and outcomes of the program." A second evaluation policy category involves *participation* in evaluation and could address how and when stakeholders are to be involved. For instance, "Evaluations will be designed with input and consultation from key program stakeholders." Three categories of policies—on capacity building, management, and roles—are related to the organizational management, resources, and infrastructure that support evaluation. A high-level *capacity building* policy might simply state "The organization will develop sufficient organizationwide capacity to support evaluation activities," with subpolicies providing more detail on what that means, such as "Staff will be trained in the methodology and use of evaluation appropriate to their program roles." *Management* policies might include policies that guide time resources ("Staff will be given sufficient time to accomplish evaluation-related activities"), policies that guide resource allocation ("Programs will allocate between 3% and 5% of total program costs for evaluation activities"), or ones that govern scheduling of evaluations ("All programs will conduct evaluations annually"). *Role* policies can be used to described the responsibilities that different people have for evaluation: "Program managers are responsible for ensuring that appropriate evaluations are conducted for each of their programs" or "Program staff are responsible for participating actively in integrating evaluation and program activities."

In the draft taxonomy all evaluation process and methods policies are collapsed into one category. To those of us who regularly work in evaluation, this may seem like too small a mechanism to contain policies that cover much of the detail about how we do our work, including question identification, sampling, measurement, design, and analysis. Perhaps so. It may be that we need several categories. Or we might subdivide this category as needed into several policy subcategories. Evaluators will see many such subdivisions, but for most nonevaluators this would be more detail than is helpful in a general taxonomy and so the broad category was used here. A *process and methods* policy might be something like "Wherever feasible, mixed methods (qualitative and quantitative) will be used in evaluations" or "Evaluation data will be stored in a secure location for no less than five years following the issuing of a report." The taxonomy includes a category for evaluation *utilization*, for instance: "Every evaluation must include a written plan for how results will be reported and used" or "Every evaluation should include an assessment of the utility of the results and recommendations for subsequent evaluations that eliminate approaches with low utility." Finally, the taxonomy includes a category for the evaluation of evaluation, or *meta-evaluation*, which could include "At least every three years the organization will contract for an independent meta-evaluation to assess the implementation, quality, and utility of its evaluations."

Notice that policies differ in their generality or specificity. An example of a broad or general "covering" policy in the process and methods category might be "Evaluations will use the highest-quality and most cost-efficient approaches and methods appropriate to the development of programs." Such general policies are essential, especially for their public and transparent signaling value, but they are not likely by themselves to be sufficient guidance for evaluation practice. They will almost always require development of subpolicies to articulate what they intend. Or another: "The highest professional standards will be used to ensure the rights and protections of evaluation participants." Notice the language here. The policy itself, at least as stated at this level, does not define what is meant by "the highest

Figure 2.2. The Evaluation Policy Wheel

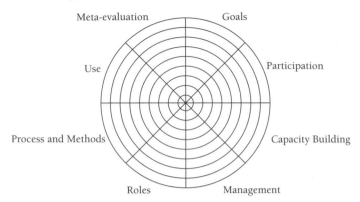

professional standards." Evaluators and other professionals have long debated what the highest professional standards are, and these are likely to evolve over time. But from a policy point of view this general covering policy plays a critical role in that it signals that organizations and units coming under the purview of this policy statement are delegated responsibility for defending how they translate or interpret the phrase "highest professional standards." Finally, it is important to note that a number of policies could legitimately be placed in multiple categories in the taxonomy. The last example could, for instance, be placed in the goals or the participants' policy category. It matters less where a particular policy is located in the taxonomy than the entire set of policies address all relevant aspects of evaluation.

Evaluation Policy Model: Structure. Our methodological framework needs a superstructure that can be used to manage complex multiple evaluation policies and their relationship to practice. The mechanism offered here is what we will call a "policy wheel," a visual rubric for policy development and evolution.[1] The policy wheel describes evaluation policy within a simple circle diagram (Figure 2.2). All evaluation policies can be located somewhere on the wheel. There are layers on the wheel, from the outermost area to the center of the circle, meant to suggest levels of generality of policy. The most general policies within their respective taxonomic categories are on the outer layers; more specific subpolicies and subsubpolicies are included in progressively inner layers. As you move to the center of the wheel, you transition from policies into practice, procedure, or operationalization. So the center of the circle is practice, and the outer layer is the highest-level policy. In effect, when you specify policies at such a level of detail that they leave no room for discretion or judgment, you are essentially prescribing the operational procedures that need to be followed.

The policy wheel is divided into eight wedges that correspond to the proposed types of evaluation policy in the taxonomy described earlier. To illustrate how the wheel is used, let's consider some hypothetical policies

Figure 2.3. Examples of Evaluation Goals and Evaluation Process and Methods Policies

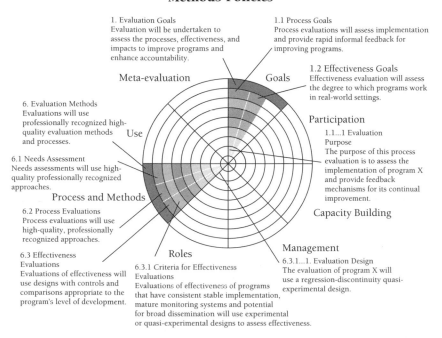

1. Evaluation Goals
Evaluation will be undertaken to assess the processes, effectiveness, and impacts to improve programs and enhance accountability.

1.1 Process Goals
Process evaluations will assess implementation and provide rapid informal feedback for improving programs.

1.2 Effectiveness Goals
Effectiveness evaluation will assess the degree to which programs work in real-world settings.

Meta-evaluation

Goals

Participation

1.1...1 Evaluation Purpose
The purpose of this process evaluation is to assess the implementation of program X and provide feedback mechanisms for its continual improvement.

6. Evaluation Methods
Evaluations will use professionally recognized high-quality evaluation methods and processes.

Use

6.1 Needs Assessment
Needs assessments will use high-quality professionally recognized approaches.

Process and Methods

Capacity Building

6.2 Process Evaluations
Process evaluations will use high-quality, professionally recognized approaches.

Management

6.3 Effectiveness Evaluations
Evaluations of effectiveness will use designs with controls and comparisons appropriate to the program's level of development.

Roles

6.3.1 Criteria for Effectiveness Evaluations
Evaluations of effectiveness of programs that have consistent stable implementation, mature monitoring systems and potential for broad dissemination will use experimental or quasi-experimental designs to assess effectiveness.

6.3.1...1. Evaluation Design
The evaluation of program X will use a regression-discontinuity quasi-experimental design.

and how they might be arrayed. These hypothetical example policies are intended to look like real policies so that we can use them to illustrate the workings of the policy methodology.

Let's begin by focusing on evaluation goals policies and consider a quick example. In the upper right portion of Figure 2.3 we see the goals policy wedge partially filled in with a hierarchy of potential evaluation policies in that area. We begin in the outer layer with the most general goal policy: "Evaluation will be undertaken to assess processes, effectiveness, and impacts to improve programs and enhance accountability." This is a very broad policy statement. There are any number of ways to make it more specific. We might want to start by specifying a more detailed policy for one aspect of this general goal, the topic of process evaluation: "Process evaluation will assess implementation and provide rapid informal feedback for improving programs." We could do more, and specify a comparable policy for effectiveness evaluation as illustrated. If we keep defining what we mean more specifically by each successive layer of policy, eventually we are going to get down to something that essentially is a description of what we will do in practice. For example, in this case we actually get to something that is essentially a description of the purpose of a process evaluation: "The purpose of this process evaluation is to assess the implementation of program X and provide feedback mechanisms for its continuous improvement."

Note that we can keep track of the policy hierarchy by numbering the policies. Because the goals policy type is the first in our taxonomy, we would number the highest-level policy in this area with a 1, the next layer of subpolicies 1.1, 1.2, and so on, until we get to something like 1.1 . . . 1 or 1.1 . . . 2 for the most detailed policies. This means we can alternatively list all of the policies in a hierarchical outline, a form that will be easier for reading them. However, the wheel is a useful visual display because it shows at a glance how specific or general the policies are across the entire taxonomy.

Consider another set of hypothetical example policies, this time in the area of process and methods policies. It begins with a general policy requiring "high-quality" evaluation methods and processes, differentiates several types of evaluation (needs assessment, process evaluation, and effectiveness evaluation), and details what constitutes high-quality methods and processes for these evaluation types. At its most specific, the example policy is essentially a prescription for what should be done under a particular set of circumstances to accomplish effectiveness evaluation—in this hypothetical example, a regression-discontinuity design, of course (Trochim, 1984)!

Evaluation Policy Model: Principles. We can also use the policy wheel as a framework for illustrating the major principles that guide the evaluation policy model (Figure 2.4). We have already seen that policies change in specificity as we move from the outer levels to the inner. This is referred to here as the principle of *specificity*. The notion that subpolicies and

Figure 2.4. Principles of the Evaluation Policy Model

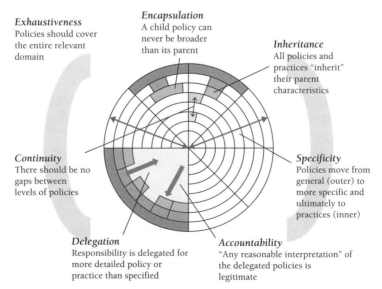

Exhaustiveness
Policies should cover the entire relevant domain

Encapsulation
A child policy can never be broader than its parent

Inheritance
All policies and practices "inherit" their parent characteristics

Continuity
There should be no gaps between levels of policies

Specificity
Policies move from general (outer) to more specific and ultimately to practices (inner)

Delegation
Responsibility is delegated for more detailed policy or practice than specified

Accountability
"Any reasonable interpretation" of the delegated policies is legitimate

ultimately practices inherit their outer-level parent policies is a principle or characteristic that can be labeled *inheritance*. That is, when you operationalize a set of policies in practice it's expected that you will enact all of the policies in the hierarchy, not just the most specifically stated one. The idea that the policy-practice continuum is hierarchical—that broader policies contain within them subpolicies, which contain within them further subpolicies—is what can be termed the principle of *encapsulation*. Policies should cover the entire relevant domain in their taxonomy and not omit anything important, a principle we might call *exhaustiveness*. There should be continuousness of specification from general policy to operational practice, or what we might call the principle of *continuity*. For instance, imagine an agency that has only one very high-level evaluation policy such as "We should have regular evaluations of all major programs" and one specific policy (almost at the level of procedure) such as "We should evaluate with randomized experiments every other Tuesday." In this hypothetical case, we are essentially jumping from a very high-level policy into something that is quite specific. Many of the controversies we encounter in real-world evaluation policy are related to this type of jump, to the lack of policy continuity. The principle of *delegation* is the idea that policies are developed to a certain level of specificity at one hierarchical level in an organization and to other levels of specificity at others. For instance, in a large, complex, multilevel organization, the broadest-level policies tend to be developed at the highest level of the hierarchy. Lower levels are delegated the responsibility of developing more specific policies appropriate for their level, with the operational staff ultimately delegated responsibility for translating policies into actual practice. Where delegation occurs, those delegated to are responsible for defending the judgments they make about how they operationalized policies, a principle we label *accountability*.

This principle of accountability is a challenging one and warrants a bit more explanation. It is based on the idea of "any reasonable interpretation" (Carver & Carver, 2006). Typically, evaluation policies are not and would not be fully specified from general policy all the way to specific practice. That is, in the real world we would never expect the policy wheel to be completely filled in. In fact, in some organizations it might be perfectly reasonable to specify only the highest-level or outer-circle policies in each area of the taxonomy and delegate responsibility to staff to determine appropriate ways to implement them. When policies are only specified to a certain level, the assumption of this model is that "any reasonable interpretation" of the most specifically stated policies would be acceptable. If you specify only a high-level process and method policy such as "Evaluations will use professionally recognized, high-quality evaluation methods and processes" and leave it at that, then any evaluation done that can be considered a reasonable interpretation of the policy should be accepted by the policy makers. Note that this puts the burden of articulating policies to the level of specificity desired on whichever person or group is responsible for policy. If an evaluation that is done meets the criterion of a reasonable interpretation of the policy but is not satisfactory to those responsible for the policy, this suggests that they need to specify more detailed levels of policy in this area. This illustrates the dynamic tension among delegation, accountability, and specificity. The less specific your policies (i.e., the more you rely on a few general policies), the more you are delegating to others the responsibility for deciding what constitutes a reasonable interpretation. Although with greater delegation staff members have greater flexibility, they also have more accountability to demonstrate that their interpretation was a reasonable one. When policies are specified in greater detail, delegation and flexibility are by definition reduced, but so is the burden or challenge of accountability.

In complex organizations or systems it is likely that policy making will itself be a hierarchical process with different levels of the hierarchical organization developing different levels of policy. High-level policies (outer circles) would be specified at the highest level of the organization, and responsibility would be delegated to subunits that inherit with those policies the responsibility for determining more detailed policies and ultimately evaluation practice. For example, consider how this might play out in the context of the U.S. federal government (Figure 2.5). At the highest level in the policy organization hierarchy—in the case of the U.S. government, this would be the Congress, which is responsible for making law—they would be expected to specify very high-level evaluation policies. The next level in

Figure 2.5. Policy in a Hierarchical Organization or System

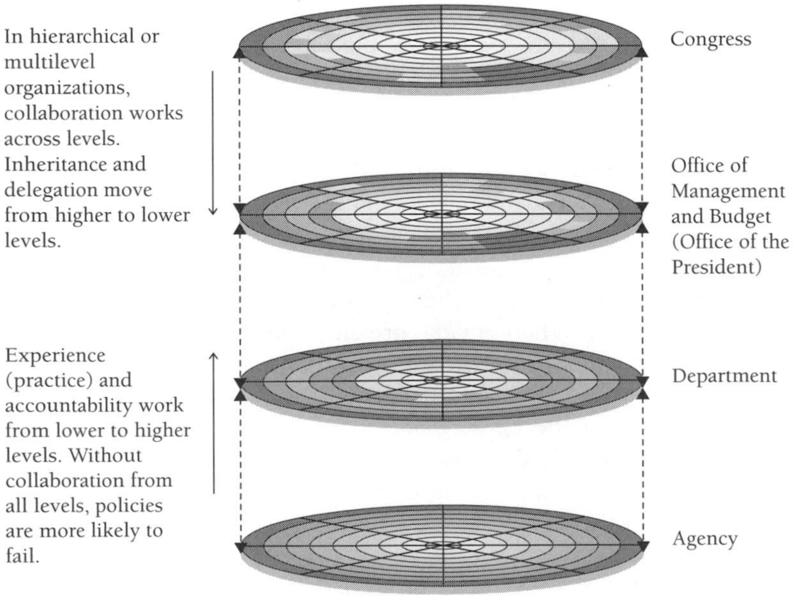

In hierarchical or multilevel organizations, collaboration works across levels. Inheritance and delegation move from higher to lower levels.

Experience (practice) and accountability work from lower to higher levels. Without collaboration from all levels, policies are more likely to fail.

Congress

Office of Management and Budget (Office of the President)

Department

Agency

the policy hierarchy might be in the Executive Branch, for instance, at the level of the Office of Management and Budget in the Office of the President. They would inherit the policies that Congress set and add more specific policies of their own. With each move further down in the hierarchy to the cabinet-level department, agency, subagency, and so on, more detail may be added into the policy wheel. At the lowest level, the "policies" are essentially short descriptions of the procedures that will be followed in conducting evaluations.

It would not be desirable for this multilevel process to be unidirectional. Certainly, policy should guide practice. But the reverse is also true: policy needs to be informed by practice. That is, we need an experiential and empirical practice base to inform policy development. Without that experiential base, policies are more likely to be ill-suited for the context and more likely to fail.

Real life seldom follows a rational model like the one offered here. For instance, if you are in a lower level of an organizational or system hierarchy (and aren't most of us?), you don't need to wait for the higher levels to formulate policy before you can develop policies at your level. Depending on where you are in the organizational structure, you can enter the policy development process at any level of this model. When you enter the hierarchy at some level and survey the existing policy landscape, you'll see that you already likely inherit a number of written or unwritten policies. And policies you help develop will likely have implications for lower levels of the hierarchy, either now or in the future.

Evaluation Policy Challenges and Opportunities

Challenges. Developing comprehensive written evaluation policies is not an easy endeavor; there will be a number of important challenges and barriers that have need to be addressed as this area develops. For instance, there is a real danger that in our zeal to articulate sensible policies we will *overformalize* the effort and develop an ineffective bureaucratized approach that actually stifles good policy making and becomes a detriment to evaluation. Finding the right balance between which policies would be specified explicitly in written form and which would evolve as implicit norms is going to be a major challenge.

Everyone who's ever worked in a large organization knows that *senseless or illogical policies* are legendary and generate a significant amount of the griping that occurs. We need research and evaluation on the effectiveness of different approaches to developing evaluation policy that help us understand how we might best avoid senseless and contradictory policies.

One of the most frustrating aspects of much organizational policy is the tendency for well-intended policies to have *unintended negative side-effects*. Unintended negative effects of policies are often the result of systems challenges; one part of the system establishes a policy that makes perfect sense to them without thinking through or realizing the negative effects it will have on another part of the system. We need to develop ways to rapidly evaluate new policies to determine when unanticipated negative effects might result.

Perhaps one of the most important challenges we are likely to face is that of *ethics*. Many of the ethical issues involved in evaluation policy have already been mentioned, including the implications of power and control issues, the importance of transparency, and the need to engage all relevant stakeholders in the policy formulation process. Evaluation policy making must be guided by our core values.

There are undoubtedly many other challenges and barriers to good evaluation policy making than just these. We will need good evaluation work to identify and catalogue such challenges and even better work to assess how best to address them.

Opportunities. It is an old adage that "with challenge comes opportunity," and this certainly is the case in the area of evaluation policy. Here are a few potential ideas evaluators might explore as we move ahead in this arena; this list might also be viewed as an agenda or a set of "next steps" to be pursued.

Evaluation Policy Audits. We desperately need descriptive studies of current evaluation policies, and this would be something we could get to work on immediately. Take a look at the evaluations you are working on and the organizations in which they are set. Determine existing evaluation practices and assess which are based on explicit written policies and which are more implicit. Conduct a systematic review of documents, including reports (such as annual reports, project reports to funders) and internal memos and communications, to identify existing evaluation policies. Relate the policies to a taxonomy, either one that already exists or one developed in the local context. Such taxonomies can in turn be used as checklists for auditing the as-is situation and suggesting potential gaps. We need to develop taxonomies and corresponding audit methodologies that are better than the ones suggested here, and these need to be informed by systematic research. For instance, research that is currently under way uses concept mapping with staff in a complex multicounty cooperative extension organization in New York State to develop a taxonomy of evaluation policies and corresponding audit procedures that would be empirically grounded (Hargraves & Trochim, 2008) and contextually appropriate.

Evaluation Working Groups for Policy Development. Very often the impetus for developing evaluation policies will arise when you are in the midst of conducting an evaluation and it becomes apparent that there is an absence of locally adopted written policies to guide your work. In such circumstances, an evaluation working group or evaluation advisory group might be a useful mechanism for initiating and facilitating an evaluation policy development effort in conjunction with ongoing evaluation. The group could be responsible for overseeing a policy audit and making recommendations for policies that need to be developed. The policies that result can then be shared with others in their organization and might form the basis of a more organizationwide subsequent policy effort.

Evaluation Policy Clearinghouses and Archives. As we begin to accomplish evaluation policy audits, it would be valuable to initiate a systematic effort to format them uniformly, archive them, and make them available publicly. Archives and clearinghouses will both encourage greater communication about policies and yield a database that would be invaluable for research, evaluation, and systematic review and synthesis, helping the field identify the most effective policies in various organizations and conditions. That is, systematic archiving would help ensure that we can be cumulative about what we learn about evaluation policy.

Evaluation Policy Analysis. More formally, we should be developing the idea of evaluation policy analysis, based on notions of the traditional field of policy analysis. One key role of such an effort would be to conduct systematic empirical comparisons of how alternative policies work and under what circumstances. If we had an archive of evaluation policies across multiple organizations, it would be possible to determine the range and types of policies in any category of the taxonomy. For instance, one of the most common questions raised by policy makers about evaluation is how much of their program budget they should allocate for evaluation. Evaluation policy analysis could look across multiple sets of policies, determine their allocations, assess the variation across contexts, and even relate them empirically to subsequent quality and efficiency of evaluations conducted.

Software Systems for Evaluation Policy Management. There is a need to develop information and software technology that can be used to help groups and organizations manage evaluation policies. For instance, we might imagine something like a Web-based software tool based on the hierarchical policy wheel of Figure 2.2. It could give complex organizations a platform for collaboratively entering and harmonizing evaluation policies throughout their systems. It could enable users to toggle back and forth between a graphic representation of policies on the wheel and a hierarchical outline of such policies. This would be an especially useful tool for very large, complex organizations where each level of the organization could enter its policies and print what is appropriate at its level while also being able to see whether there are gaps in policy specification or how their policies compare with what other groups in the organization are doing.

Consulting on Evaluation Policy. There's a potential cottage industry out there for evaluation consultants in connection with evaluation policy. One can imagine evaluation policy consultants who are contracted by organizations to facilitate development and management of their evaluation policies, who would be responsible for managing policy audits, reviewing potential policies from other similar organizations, archiving the policies that are developed, and so on. Here's where evaluators' extensive knowledge of both the field of evaluation and of participatory and facilitative methods could be put to good use to enhance evaluation policy.

Harmonizing Evaluation and Other Policies. It is important to recognize that evaluation does not exist in a vacuum. Although this chapter has focused on evaluation policy, most organizations already have (sometimes extensive) written policies to cover everything from personnel management to acquisitions and contracting, to strategic planning and finance. Evaluation policies need to be integrated into the larger organizational policy framework that already likely exists. This means that evaluators must become more familiar with the methodologies and structures for developing traditional policy and procedure manuals in organizations and ensure that our work can be integrated appropriately.

Conclusions. A central message of this chapter is that we have to be more serious about evaluation policy. We have to encourage more written, public, and transparent evaluation policies. We have to develop a balance between the desire for general policies that cover an organization consistently and the need for flexibility and adaptation. We have to address and acknowledge the issues of power, hierarchy, delegation, and incentive; encourage collaboration and participation; and encourage archiving and sharing of policies.

Perhaps it's fitting to conclude by recalling that evaluation policy is important because it guides evaluation practice, which in turn influences the quality of the programs and policies that shape people's lives. For many evaluators, providing compelling analysis of and practical suggestions for improving public policies and programs is one of the best ways we can enhance our society. In the United States we are at an especially important moment with the change in Washington to the Obama administration, which faces a national debt in the trillions of dollars, annual deficits in the hundreds of billions, and uncertainties about financial institutions and the economy. At the same time, concerns remain about national security, health care, education, energy development, and many other facets of American life (AEA Evaluation Policy Task Force, 2009).

To the Obama administration we need to say that program evaluation is essential to addressing these issues. It can help answer new questions about current and emerging problems, reduce wasteful spending, increase accountability, and support major decisions about program reforms and improvements. President Obama has pledged to review all government programs to identify those that work and those that don't, and to make vital programs work better than they do now. We need to encourage the new administration to examine not just government programs but also how it evaluates them. We need to help key political appointees and senior careerists in the Executive Branch and the Congress to make program evaluation integral to managing government programs at all stages, from initial development through startup, ongoing implementation, and reauthorization. A more concerted and coherent effort to develop sensible evaluation policies, to archive and make them available to others, and to conduct evaluations to assess their effectiveness is critically important to making an effective case for evaluation in the Obama administration and in the future.

Note

1. Several key features of this model are adapted from the work of John and Miriam Carver on the governance policies for boards of directors of organizations (Carver, 2006; Carver & Carver, 2006). The unique needs of evaluation policy required adaptations and considerable extensions to these features, which undoubtedly distort or change them, hopefully appropriately for this context. The methodology offered here owes a clear debt to their work, but the Carvers should bear none of the responsibility for the faults of these adaptations.

References

AEA Evaluation Policy Task Force. (2008). *Comments on "What constitutes strong evidence of a program's effectiveness?"* Retrieved March 19, 2009, from http://www.eval.org/aea08.omb.guidance.responseF.pdf

AEA Evaluation Policy Task Force. (2009). *An evaluation roadmap for a more effective government.* Retrieved March 19, 2009, from http://www.eval.org/aea09.eptf.eval.roadmapF.pdf

Carver, J. (2006). *Boards that make a difference.* San Francisco: Jossey-Bass.

Carver, J., & Carver, M. (2006). *Reinventing your board: A step-by-step guide to implementing policy governance.* San Francisco: Jossey-Bass.

Chen, H., & Rossi, P. (1990). *Theory-driven evaluations.* Thousand Oaks, CA: Sage.

Cousins, J. B., & Whitmore, E. (1998). Framing participatory evaluation. *New Directions for Evaluation, 80,* 5–23.

Fetterman, D., Kaftarian, S. J., & Wandersman, A. (1996). *Empowerment evaluation: Knowledge and tools for self-assessment and accountability.* Thousand Oaks, CA: Sage.

Hargraves, M., & Trochim, W. (2008, November). *Designing and implementing evaluation policies to sustain evaluation practice in extension programs.* Paper presented at the Annual Conference of the American Evaluation Association, Denver, Colorado.

Julnes, G., & Rog, D. (Eds.). (2007). Informing federal policies on evaluation methodology: Building the evidence base for method choice in government sponsored evaluation. *New Directions in Evaluation, 113.*

Kane, M., & Trochim, W. (2006). *Concept mapping for planning and evaluation.* Thousand Oaks, CA: Sage.

King, J. A. (1998). Making sense of participatory evaluation practice. *New Directions for Evaluation, 80,* 57–67.

Patton, M. Q. (2008). *Utilization-focused evaluation* (4th ed.). London: Sage.

Preskill, H. (2007, November). *Evaluation's second act: A spotlight on learning.* Paper presented at the 2007 Annual Conference of the American Evaluation Association, Denver, Colorado.

Trochim, W. (1984). *Research design for program evaluation: The regression-discontinuity approach.* Thousand Oaks, CA: Sage.

Trochim, W. (Ed.). (1989). *Concept mapping for evaluation and planning* (Vol. 12, 1). New York: Pergamon.

Trochim, W., & Kane, M. (2005). Concept mapping: An introduction to structured conceptualization in health care. *International Journal for Quality in Health Care, 17*(3), 187–191.

U.S. Department of Education. (2003, November 4). Scientifically based evaluation methods. *Federal Register,* 62445–62447.

WILLIAM M. K. TROCHIM *is professor of policy analysis and management at Cornell University and the director of evaluation for the Weill Cornell Clinical and Translational Science Center, the director of evaluation for extension and outreach, and the director of the Cornell Office for Research on Evaluation.*

NEW DIRECTIONS FOR EVALUATION • DOI: 10.1002/ev

Datta, L.-e. (2009). Golden is the sand: Memory and hope in evaluation policy and evaluation practice. In W.M.K. Trochim, M. M. Mark, & L. J. Cooksy (Eds.), *Evaluation policy and evaluation practice. New Directions for Evaluation, 123*, 33–50.

3

Golden Is the Sand: Memory and Hope in Evaluation Policy and Evaluation Practice

Lois-ellin Datta

Abstract

Going from thought to action in influencing evaluation policy is an overdue, untried, and perhaps anxious-making role for the American Evaluation Association. We will need good courage, sustained conversation, and the widest views. The courage is needed in remembering that although this isn't going to be fast or easy, evaluation policies make a big enough difference to be worth a big effort. Sustained conversation is needed to find the common ground that exists in practice, while perhaps trying a little benign neglect of the diversity that exists in theoretical stances. Widest views that include in-depth understanding of globalization and other broad changes are needed so our policies can be appropriate for the half-century ahead, rather than the 50 years past. © Wiley Periodicals, Inc.

Note: Many thanks to Jonathan Bruel, Valerie Caracelli, Leslie Cooksy, George Grob, Michael Hendricks, Anna Lobosco, Jules Marquart, Mel Mark, and Bill Trochim for their helpful comments.

NEW DIRECTIONS FOR EVALUATION, no. 123, Fall 2009 © Wiley Periodicals, Inc., and the American Evaluation Association. Published online in Wiley InterScience (www.interscience.wiley.com) • DOI: 10.1002/ev.304

Consider these two images: boats on a river and a pushmi-pullyu. The boats on the river are evaluation policies the American Evaluation Association hopes to influence. I see these as boats the present launches, that on down the river the future will bring ashore. How can we launch these boats with a strong heart? Of what might they consist? How do we get them floating?

Dr. Dolittle's pushmi-pullyu is a llamalike animal with a head on each end that can look inward at itself and outward. It gets along by cooperatively pushing and pulling in the same direction. In the pushmi-pullyu, I see our evaluation policies now being shaped primarily by the inner gaze, which is all very well if not necessarily always very harmonious. Nevertheless, the creature needs to consider an outer gaze as well. To use another metaphor, if no man is an island, then neither should evaluation policy be separate from the mainland of what else is happening as memory and hope once again battle it out.

Working within this framework, we perhaps can hold these truths to be partly self-evident: evaluation policies are important, organizations can influence evaluation policy, and we need to welcome wide representation from the evaluation field. The next sections elaborate the why and how of these ideas, which may sound "motherpie" and "applehood," but which can be challenging to carry out.

Evaluation Policies Are Important

Once upon a time, not so long ago, our country began a grand transformation. We had survived the agony of the 1930s Great Depression. With our Allies, we prevailed in World War II. After that war, the world slowly and often painfully rebuilt itself. Children were born to parents determined to shield them from the dark at the top of the stairs. Then, gathering courage from many sources, we began to want a better life for all Americans. On August 28, 1963, my kids, a tank of trained tilapia fish, and I, immigrants from Pennsylvania, roasted in a massive traffic jam by the Lincoln Memorial as we heard for the first time the words "I have a dream."

Evaluation has been a part of that dream. Evaluation as we know it began in the 1960s. From the memories of bad times came requirements for finding out, on a broad scale, if the Great Society initiatives were worthwhile. From hope that empowering the disenfranchised could lead to enduring change came Robert F. Kennedy's dogged insistence on local control of local knowledge in the evaluation provisions of the Elementary and Secondary Education Act of 1965.

Academics, practitioners, and policy makers worked together. The evaluation policies of the 1960s and 1970s grew from the confluence of political needs and professorial knowledge. The professors came to Washington, stayed a while, influenced and were influenced by the experience, and then returned. Their students become evaluation policy makers and influencers; their grandstudents are today's and tomorrow's evaluation leaders.

Our evaluation profession has long rejoiced in illustrious individuals who affect evaluation policy, sometimes as members of panels, sometimes through organizations in their special areas: health, justice, environment, public health, housing, and education. In 2007, for the first time, the American Evaluation Association decided to stand forth to represent what we, its members, believe to be important for evaluation policies and practice as they are expressed in legislation, regulations, and expenditures. Initially, this has meant federal evaluation policies. AEA aspires to be a recognized player in evaluation policy, initiating what we ourselves see as sound evaluation policy and equally supporting sound evaluation policies initiated by others. This also means, if necessary, using our influence to avoid or correct evaluation policies that seem to us unsound. Arguably, it is this latter role that propelled us across the border between organizational determination and organizational reticence.

Continuing and developing conversations to this end was the theme of our 2008 conference, auspiciously beginning at what could fairly be called a time of accelerating hope. We should expect gradual influence, however, rather than sudden changes in evaluation policies. Rarely does a new administration operate through a slew of executive orders, and legislation is rarely swift. Further, we are playing catch-up. Some highly influential organizations such as the Brookings Institution, for instance, have much appreciation for science-based evaluation but little discernible leadership for more diverse approaches. Perhaps more rapid changes may come through appointments to cabinet and subcabinet positions, particularly, in our case, positions associated with evaluation leadership. Slow can seem unsteady, but nonetheless policies do make a difference and organizations such as AEA can affect them.

Never doubt that policies make a difference. A story: HIV/AIDS—the virus, the bad guy—has been holding its own against the best of us who are intent on its obliteration. More precisely, treatment access, survival, and quality of life have improved. New-infection rates in subgroups such as younger African American men generally have not improved. The quest continues for new paradigms for preventing infection. Shifting from individual outreach to broad-based community efforts looks promising. In 2008, about 30 of us heard about these initiatives, being asked if, how, and to what extent evaluation paradigms should shift too (San Francisco Aids Foundation, 2008).

We may wonder about the difference evaluation policy really makes to evaluation practice and whether we can work within most evaluation policies even when they seem inappropriately constricting or insufficiently prescriptive. The stance of one experienced, brilliant, hard-working, and caring researcher in this meeting showed how difficult this can be. We had been discussing evaluation models based on systems approaches. The ideas seemed appropriate to the broad-based community initiatives. Ruefully,

NEW DIRECTIONS FOR EVALUATION • DOI: 10.1002/ev

the researcher said, "There is no way I can propose this. It would never get funded." His comment is echoed by another experienced HIV evaluator: "Tell them how evaluation methods are being narrowed." Others, I recognize, would say, "Improved."

Another instance is discussed by Cahalan (2008), as a PART tragedy in the case of Upward Bound. As seen by Cahalan, concerns with design were raised early but ignored by the Institute for Educational Science, resulting in a PART rating of ineffective and consequent zero funding of federal pre-college programs. The concerns centered on an evaluation policy mandating use of intent-to-treat (ITT) analyses despite what Cahalan sees as compelling evidence of biases favoring the control group and evidence showing program effectiveness when defensible alternative analyses such as treatment-on-treated were used. The policy regarding ITT remains in effect as of this writing.

Evaluation policies—real or perceived—affect what is funded, but more importantly they ultimately affect beliefs about the value of programs. We surely wish to establish the best boundaries. This requires good conversation about what is appropriate in what circumstances. Our stances on specific evaluation policies should be shaped through the internal gaze—evaluators examining evaluation issues—and equally, through the external gaze. By this, I mean our awareness of great movements in our social, economic, and political worlds—what is happening inside our house, yes; but also what's happening outside.

The Role Organizations Can Have in Influencing Policy: Boldly Building Our Evaluation Policy Boats

The AEA Policy Task Force (2007) identifies seven areas of evaluation policy. Paraphrasing from the Task Force charge, these dimensions are:

1. Evaluation definition: How is evaluation defined in an agency or legislation? How is evaluation formally distinguished from functions such as program planning, monitoring, and performance measurement?
2. Requirements of evaluation: When are evaluations required, what programs should have evaluations, how often are evaluations scheduled?
3. Evaluation methods: Approaches recommended or required for different types of programs.
4. Human resources: Types of training, experience, and background required for evaluators.
5. Evaluation budgets: Standards for budgeting evaluation work.
6. Evaluation implementation: Guidance on how evaluation should be carried out, for example, the definitions of internal and external evaluation and when they are required. Where should evaluation units be located to balance knowledge and independence?
7. Evaluation ethics: Policies for addressing ethical issues in evaluation.

To these seven dimensions of policy, I would add two more dimensions:

8. Who is involved: Are AEA evaluators part of the discussions? How is diversity of approaches within evaluation represented in panels, workshops, and other policy-and-practice influencing bodies? By diversity, I mean *arenas of practice* such as academic and applied and *locus of practice* such as local, state, federal, and nonprofits, as well as ethnic, racial, and cultural diversity. "Federal" is a beginning, but it cannot be an end.

9. Resource distributions: How exclusively or inclusively with regard to evaluation perspectives are resources directed for evaluation training, publications, fellowships, conferences, and other capacity-building efforts?

Trochim, in Chapter 2, offers more elaborated dimensions. These fine-grained dimensions may be valuable for research on evaluation policies or tracing the transformation from unwritten, specific policies to written evaluation guidance. Those of the AEA Task Force seem to me to be at quite a useful level for focusing our limited energies.

These dimensions can be influenced by organizations, as illustrated by the justifiable pride seen when an evaluation group can claim direct credit for getting evaluation requirements into a law. For example, one organization claims responsibility for the wording in the Second Chance Act (Public Law 110–199):

> which per our input contains a 2% set-aside for rigorous evaluations of strategies to facilitate prisoner re-entry into the community. Specifically, the Act contains a provision that we helped develop to set aside 2% of the program funds for evaluations that "include, to the maximum extent feasible, random assignment . . . and generate evidence on which re-entry approaches and strategies are most effective."

From the same organization:

> Our work with Congress and OMB helped create a new $10 million evidence-based home visitation program in the FY08 Appropriations Act (Public Law 110–161). Based on our input, the final Congressional language directs the Department of Health and Human Services to "ensure that states use funds to support models that have been shown in well-designed randomized controlled trials, to produce sizeable, sustained effects on important child outcomes such as abuse and neglect."
>
> (Both from the Coalition for Evidence-Based Policy of
> the Council for Excellence in Government, 2008)

Or, continuing the examples of pride in informing evaluation policy, the American Evaluation Association (2008) reports that after a meeting

NEW DIRECTIONS FOR EVALUATION • DOI: 10.1002/ev

with the director of the Office of Management and Budget, AEA was invited to comment on the evaluation guidelines in the OMB document "What Constitutes Strong Evidence of a Program's Effectiveness?" and to provide seminars and workshops on views expressed in our association's comments to OMB staff. OMB is said to be initiating a pilot test using guidelines suggested by AEA to assess evidence of program effectiveness. This could be a valuable example of AEA's role in improving or correcting evaluation policies developed by others.

Another instance may be helpful. This one has to do with researcher and evaluator training. For many years, fellowships to grow the next generation of researchers were managed by organizations such as the National Academy of Education and the National Science Foundation. In the area of education, much of the funding came from the U.S. Department of Education, the Institute of Education Sciences. I use the past tense. These funds have been redirected. In 2007–08, the money was consolidated into the department's programs to support graduate training to carry out "the new rigorous evaluation mandates in federal legislation," accompanying Institute of Education Sciences' initiation of an educational evaluation journal publishing only work related to these mandates (Viadero, 2008a). This makes excellent policy sense. If federal leaders believe in the primacy of randomized experimentation, they will want to use federal funds to establish publications and journals, train the rising generation of evaluators in these social experimentation techniques, underwrite conferences, and establish graduate research institutes, faculty, and programs dedicated to these approaches (Viadero, 2008b). Previous administrations did much the same thing, for example, in promoting the 1970s–1980s focus on gender equity.

These are examples of what I mean by policies and by efforts to influence evaluation policies. I applaud the AEA Evaluation Policy Task Force's efforts to educate OMB but prefer the more direct action of legislative requirements: drafting, influencing, shaping, and growing what evaluation policy we want in our laws, and greater attention also to evaluation funding. The growing popularity of evaluation mandates has yielded a flourishing profession, but I worry about the quality of evaluations and their actual value, when adequate money is not available. As I heard during the 2008 conference, our Policy Task Force is already moving in the direction of a wider scope of influence.

Efforts to influence policies are daily bread. It is why we elect some people and not others to implement these policies and not those. Women and men running the agencies do their best to carry out the policies. Groups who want their voices heard have to speak up. As noted above, this is appropriate, and nothing new to many groups. It is we in AEA who have been reticent and out of touch. That is, we have missed opportunities—an issue that I hope is now being corrected.

NEW DIRECTIONS FOR EVALUATION • DOI: 10.1002/ev

For instance, over a hundred social science organizations work through an advocacy group, the Consortium of Social Science Organizations (COSSA). AEA is not currently one of them. In 2007 and 2008, COSSA's testimonies focused on support for research budgets. COSSA would be likely, in my view, to get involved in evaluation policy areas such as budgets were we to ask them, but unlikely to get involved in more technical areas such as methodology.

A second instance: I contacted the active and effective Center on Education Policy. The center has testified and lobbied with vigor on many aspects of education-related legislation. However, this powerful and well-connected council has also not testified or prepared recommendations on evaluation policy. They also might be willing to get involved in evaluation policy, were we to ask them. If we consider lightning-rod issues of evaluation design and assessment in education policy, our reticence here in forming alliances with policy groups seems almost amazing.

Third, we are absent from too many tables. For example, a 2007 evaluation policy initiative for early childhood education involved more than 58 people, not one of whom—as far as I know—is a member of AEA, and AEA was not officially represented. As another example, EVALTALK has acres of discussions such as the political motivations for high-stakes testing. I have yet to see a thread discussing a specific legislative provision relating to evaluation, although, to be sure, there were mega-messages (bordering on rants) about the U.S. Department of Education guidelines on evidence of effectiveness. Lastly and alas-ly, as a small indicator of possibly inadequate knowledge of specific evaluation-policy-related legislative provisions, my personal request on four evaluation listservs for evaluation-relevant legislation yielded no, zero, nada responses. I think we care, but we do not know much about the road to legislation. Those wishing more information on this path will find riches in both Thomas (http://thomas.loc.gov/), a site of the U.S. Congress on bills under consideration, and the U.S. Government Printing Office, on bills signed into law.

So, influencing evaluation policy really is a new role for AEA. We have not been around much when evaluation policies are written. To reiterate, what is written into legislation and what is reified in regulations and deified in guidance affects how I practice evaluation and probably how you practice it too, at least to some degree.

What should these policies be? Who decides what evaluation policies the American Evaluation Association promotes? These have been among the sticking points in the past and are part of some well-argued reasons policy influencing should be a road not taken by AEA. We begin, I think, with some fear and trembling. It can be tough to construct evaluation policies that honor the diversity of our field yet are specific enough to be policy useful. How do we decide, as a diverse group, what policies we want to promote?

NEW DIRECTIONS FOR EVALUATION • DOI: 10.1002/ev

Who Needs to Be at the Table? The Value of Wider Representation From the Evaluation Field

Consider first the inward gaze of the pushmi-pullyu. Much sense of what evaluation policies should be comes from debated issues of our profession. Since 1986, three of our national conventions have had policy as a theme. These were Michael Quinn Patton's 1988 theme of Evaluation and Politics, Yvonna Lincoln's 1990 theme of Evaluation and the Formulation of Public Policy, and our 2008 conference, led by President Bill Trochim. Two others could be considered related to policy: Mel Mark's 2006 theme of the Consequences of Evaluation and Molly Engle's 2002 Evaluation—A Systematic Process That Reforms Systems. The themes led to discussions of how evaluation results affect program policy and how policy and politics influence evaluation.

Some of the sessions have yielded reports related to what evaluation policies our association might promote. One example is the *New Directions for Evaluation* (2007) issue edited by George Julnes and Debra Rog, "Informing Federal Policies on Evaluation Methodology: Building the Evidence Base for Method Choice in Government Sponsored Evaluation."

With the stalwart exception of methodology, I could not find, however, systematic examination of where our association and its members stood on the other eight evaluation policy dimensions. When we talk about policy, it is often how the processes and results of evaluation affect programs— evaluation utilization—more than how evaluators should affect evaluation policies. Among the exceptions are Eleanor Chelimsky's eloquent calls for courage, her efforts to enlighten our political naïveté, and her superb analyses of the highly significant policy issues with regard to positioning evaluation units to achieve independence (Chelimsky, 2008, and this issue).

Therefore, I am extrapolating. Returning to the dimensions, suppose we did a poll now on what our policy stances should be. I see probable unanimity in six, possible unanimity in two, and "maybe we can get there" in one.

Unanimity, or at least reasonably close agreement, seems likely in:

- The *definitions* of what evaluation is, compared (for instance) to program monitoring.
- The *requirements* for evaluation: when evaluations are appropriate and should be done.
- *Human resources*
- *Budgets*—good evaluations take money and time, and they should be funded when evaluations are required or mandated. We probably could come to agreement on reasonable set-asides.
- *Evaluation implementation*, what carrying out a sound evaluation means.
- *Ethics* is another area where we probably could reach agreement— and indeed have, if the American Evaluation Association Guidelines and

discussions of ethics in leading books by evaluators of many persuasions are indicators.

For example, most evaluators seem likely to distinguish among evaluations for program improvement, formative, or process evaluations; think they are useful; see them as appropriate during start-up phases of a program; and agree that a program should be, in Tom Cook's wonderful phrase, "proud and mature" before impact or summative evaluations are undertaken. We might have variations on how to do the formative evaluations and what evidence might indicate readiness for summative evaluations, but our field could reach some reasonable policy position on these points.

In contrast, possible unanimity after continuing discussions within our profession seem likely in:

- *Involvement*—the necessity or not for diverse participation in evaluation policy planning
- *Resource distribution diversity*—in appropriateness or not of concentrating federal evaluation capacity building funds on one or a few approaches

Finally, maybe we can get there, in my view, with regard to what *methodologies* are appropriate for estimating effects and establishing attribution. For example, in the first issues of the journal of the Society for Research on Educational Effectiveness (SREE), most of the articles dealing with impact found that the randomized designs yielded no effects findings *until degree of implementation was taken into account.* Many of us have been talking for years about the necessity of finding out what is actually happening in interventions, both for intended focal and comparison groups and for using data to learn what leads to what, regardless of the aegis or label under which the experiences happened. We may have reached a point of no return in debate on principles and theory and could make notable progress if we focused on looking at our common wisdom as shown in actual evaluation practice.

Others may be less sanguine regarding the likelihood of agreement on issues such as methods for estimating effects. Granted, debates have been ferocious, but I rather hold with R. K. Merton, that lovely scholar of the philosophy of science. Merton (1965) first cites Newton's letter to Hook: "What's done before many witnesses is seldom without some further concern than that for truth; but what passes between friends in private usually deserves ye name of consultation rather than contest" (p. 23). Then Merton delightedly cites himself: "These controversies [referring to debates in sociology] follow the classically identified course of social conflict. Attack is followed by counter-attack, with progressive alienation of each party to the conflict. Since the conflict becomes public, it becomes a battle for status more nearly than a search for truth" (pp. 24–25). I propose we have some get-togethers looking at specific evaluations such as those published in SREE and AEA journals that have productively used similar methods for taking experience into account, and see if we can formulate some wise general approaches for policy. After all, we already have done so in much practice.

Further, international organizations may be moving toward more nuanced statements. In the United States, there is still currently public and rather alienating disagreement on the definition of appropriate methodologies. Some of us believe that when the purpose is estimating program impact, there is a hierarchy of increasingly more convincing approaches, and evaluation policy should be to go for the gold or not at all (Coalition for Evidence-Based Policy, 2008). Some of us believe that when the purpose is estimating program impact, there is a platinum standard of appropriate methodologies that are context-dependent.

Statements such as White's representing the influential new international evaluation organization, 3ie (White, 2008), and those of the European Evaluation Society (2007) seem consistent with this latter view. Further, the bloom may be slightly off the strict constructionist view of the experimentation rose (intent-to-treat analyses) as a result of instances such as the $40 million evaluation of the $6 billion federal Reading First program coming up macro-negative in a stringent randomized design, a study criticized (in part) because "it did not consider the likelihood that Reading First principles and practices have spread to schools outside the program."

This is just my take. I think a much better empirically based analysis of each of the seven or nine dimensions should be considered as our association takes a stance of influencing evaluation policies, be they international, federal, state, local, or private sector.

A worthy achievement. If my hunches are reasonable, we should feel good about having agreement in so many areas. It is a worthy achievement as a profession that is about 30 to 40 years old to find consensus on how evaluation is distinct from and related to other efforts. It is a worthy achievement, reading across a variety of books and articles, to find consistent guidance for properly carrying out evaluations. Stakeholder involvement, for example, seems discussed in books from many evaluation perspectives, as does due care in data collection and reporting. I have not seen much on budgets, other than concurrence that unfunded mandates make life difficult for program directors. A 2% set-aside for evaluation can be fine, if the result is large enough for the work required; so could a 4% set-aside, such as what the U.S. Department of Health and Human Services enjoys; so could a rough rule of thumb of $10 million annually for a large multisite project. Wise ethical guidance is found in books and articles from evaluators of many theoretical and philosophical persuasions. We need to remember and remember and remember that all evaluators care about social justice, about finding approaches to help improve the human condition, and about respecting others. In my view, no one group or groups of evaluators can claim the moral high ground by the greater purity of its intentions, theory, or practice.

I think we need more empirical data to bolster the theory-based claims of different perspectives. We could benefit from better empirical evidence demonstrating the claimed merits of some of the alternative approaches taken to scale for the purpose of estimating program <u>impact</u>. We could benefit, in my view, equally from a deeper look at whether—in practice—the randomized control trial turns out to be robust or too often compromised by the expedients needed to deal with post-assignment situations (Darling-Hammond & Youngs, 2002).

It is healthy to keep on, as we are, with discussions based on theory and hope, while experience is gathered. Until then, however, the American Evaluation Association and others will need to be as specific as possible, in my view, in describing whether evidence or theory is the primary basis for claims about methodological approaches, the circumstances under which each would be honored in policy development, and the uncertainties as well as hoped-for benefits—in Julnes and Rog's terms, the evidence basis and the theory basis for federal evaluation policies.

The Pushmi-pullyu Looks Outward: The Party of Memory and the Party of Hope

Consider now the external gaze and the importance of wider—the widest—representation as evaluation policy develops, including the wider world, with its longer cycles of polarities and tensions. Some consider the best analogy to be changing course for an aircraft carrier, a ponderous operation and mechanical. I prefer the analogy of the dark-brown river of the song, flowing over golden sands, curving its new road adaptively.

Neither the metaphor nor the polarities are new. Schlesinger (1986) discussed a 30-year cycle shifting between public action and private interest, between reform and consolidation, between eras of public action and those of private interest. In 1919, Henry Adams saw a similar 12-year swing of a pendulum in the early years of our country (Adams & Adams, 1919). Ralph Waldo Emerson spoke in 1841 of the poles of hope and memory, of innovation and conservatism, each with its merits, each its limitations. He said:

> The two parties which divide the state . . . are very old and have disputed possession of the world ever since it was made. The war rages not only on battlefields, in national councils, and ecclesiastical synods, but agitates every man's bosom with opposing advantages every hour. On rolls the old world meantime, and now one, now the other gets the day, and still the fight renews itself as if for the first time, under new names and hot personalities. Such an . . . antagonism must have a correspondent depth of seat in the human constitution. It is the opposition of Past and Future, of Memory and Hope, of Understanding and Reason.

NEW DIRECTIONS FOR EVALUATION • DOI: 10.1002/ev

Where do things stand today? Are the claims of memory and of hope at equilibrium, or as some argue at a tipping point? These claims form the larger picture within which are situated the forces affecting broad habits of mind, large changes in the currents of resources and priorities and of the nature of evaluation.

I invite us to consider specific changes that are redefining our world, as summarized in Table 3.1. As seen by Zakaria (2008) and the National Intelligence Council (2008), among many others, they include economic, social, and environmental shifts.

Let us look at just two of these big changes and why evaluation policies should look outward at them. First, consider globalized markets. Many outcomes with which we deal as evaluators have to do with economic

Table 3.1. The Outward View: Examples of Global Shifts Redefining Our World

From	To
Internal or trading partner markets	Global markets
Older world powers, primarily Russia and the United States	New world powers, including China and India; redistribution of economic, industrial, financial, educational, and social dominance: "the rise of the rest"
Climate stability	Rapid climate deterioration
Population shifts generally gradual	Mass migrations
In the club, weapons of mass destruction	Proliferation of weapons of mass destruction
Relatively contained health threats	Viral pandemics
Relatively slow communications, inward	Instant, worldwide communications, outward
National autonomy	Economic and defense aggregates
Linguistic, religious, and history-based political entities	Global interest-based communities
Stable nations	Failing states
Identifiable enemies	Changing nature of war
Unipolar world influence in economic, industrial, financial, education, social, and politico-military dominance	Multipolarity
Centralized	Decentralized and interconnected
Concentration of wealth in Western world	Dispersion of global wealth and power to East
Primacy of state actors in armed conflicts	Growing influence of nonstate actors
U.S. military leadership	Coalitions

well-being. Many of the international projects we may be called on to evaluate have economic well-being as the driver of other changes. I do not think we can sensibly evaluate such projects in a local context. To understand these outcomes related to economic well-being in a world whose markets are increasingly globalized, evaluators will need a firmer grasp than most of us have on how these markets operate, what may impede or facilitate the projects, and which indicators are more or less interpretable. The assertion by analogy that one does not need to know how an internal combustion engine works to evaluate automotive performance may be too limited because as evaluators we may increasingly seek understanding of what is happening beyond outcomes per se. If this is so, then there are many policy dimensions where we should look at the language of legislation, regulation, and guidance. To mention only two: evaluation capacity building resources and methodological considerations, particularly opening the door to systems-based approaches and incorporating deeper understanding of the tensions among globalized, regional, state, and local markets (see White, 2008; National Center for Education Evaluation and Regional Assistance, 2003; American Evaluation Association, 2008).

As a small example of legislative wording going from this thought into policy action, consider a provision in the hypothetical PL 09-01, the New Economic Recovery Act: "$50,000,000 shall be made available for graduate fellowships on evaluating effects of these programs in health, education, agriculture, and energy from a global perspective."

Second, consider new world powers. Chinese studies may be among the growth industries in our universities. The term *new world powers* often refers to China and India. It also is shorthand for the awakening potential giants in Africa and South America, both of which may have natural resources that in the future will supplant petroleum-based economies. Some, for example, predict water will be the new oil before long. If this is so, then among the policies related to conduct of evaluations and to ethics might be this modest eight-word reminder: "Culturally appropriate measures and methods shall be included."

A few words can unpack into more complex initiatives. For instance, evaluator training might routinely include internships in these new world powers. This could continue awareness raising and workshop sessions already widely available, but it implies more than a unilateral suggestion. It implies an international effort to examine national evaluation policies that appropriately would incorporate awareness of "the rise of the rest" and new world powers. To the extent possible, these policies would be internationally coordinated and consistent in supporting how evaluation is done. Further, my point implies experiential learning, through training our graduate students by their participation in carrying out international and cross-national studies and their time living in diverse countries as evaluators-in-training.

Our colleagues in the Aotearoa/New Zealand Evaluation Association have been leaders in examining culturally appropriate evaluations, as have our own AEA International and Cross-Cultural, Multicultural, and Indigenous Peoples Topical Interest Groups. The African Evaluation Association has been eloquent with regard to this issue. It follows, in my opinion, equally, that the American Evaluation Association should continue ever more energetically in coordinating its evaluation policy efforts with those of IDEA, IOCE, 3ie, and other international groups. We must work within our own polity, but we must do so with the fullest possible awareness and discourse with other groups.

The Party of Memory. These two instances may or may not be the first that you think of in gazing outward. Further, others talk less positively about policies that might let us negotiate well the current and future situations, and we need to be aware of these more sorrowful possibilities. For example, Kagan (2008) argues that the post–Cold War is much the same old, same old—a complicated and dangerous place, fraught with nationalism and religious fanaticism, with predominant geopolitical rivalries between the autocracies, seen as Russia and China, and the democracies, seen as the United States, Europe, and Japan. Kagan offers an antidote to what might be overly optimistic thinking and the premature embrace of a global perspective. The policy implications of what could and should be done he leaves to others, but his views offer an analytic basis for doctrines such as preemptive warfare and establishment of a "League of Democracies." These views are embodied in the positions of one of our political parties and can be expected to be part of future dialogue. Whoever prevails, evaluation policy should be aware of these larger currents.

The Post-AEA World. At least some of the changes described for the world and for the United States apply to the American Evaluation Association. AEA has been a leader whose exports included concepts, theories, books, and marvelous flying professors. We still are exporters, as asking about last year's international travels for our AEA leaders quickly demonstrates.

Granted, we are increasingly importing, as we should, evaluation leaders and ideas from other countries, yet our gaze too often has been inward, examining in lapidary detail differences in evaluation thought within AEA. Forget it. Our gaze must be increasingly outward, and we will have to run faster than the Red Queen to keep up with evaluation ideas and developments emerging around the world. We have been the preeminent intellectual home for evaluators, never entirely, but generally. Get over it. Evaluation policies have been formulated already by organizations around the world, and we can learn from those developed, for example, by the European Evaluation Society, UNICEF, and the International Initiative for Impact Evaluations.

Even in the United States, some—perhaps many—evaluators find their intellectual home in their professional domain. Others find their home along methodological fault lines. We are dispersed, and the conversations of our diaspora are too sporadic and too few. Within AEA, we may hardly know of the major national evaluations undertaken by such groups as the Urban Institute, Westat, Mathematica, and Abt Associates. Their evaluation staff may have little knowledge of evaluations at state, local, and foundational sources.

Our association is adapting to these and other changes. We are keenly aware, for example, that much evaluator training now takes place in workshops and institutes and presessions. We have collaborated with the Centers for Disease Control. We have helped distribute information about the Evaluators' Institute. We offer splendid presessions. We need to do more.

Are these the only (or even the most significant) dimensions of this time of memory and of hope for our world, for our country, and for our association? Surely not, and during the coming months and years we will continue what we do well: think and talk. Let us talk about methodology, let us look at techniques such as influence mapping (ODI, 2008) that suggest strategies for going from thought to action, and let us talk about larger changes during discussion of how to be a significant voice in conversation about evaluation policy. I honor the leadership of those who will take us forward and those who have said for many years—eloquently and loudly—that AEA must be among those voices. Let us particularly applaud Michael Scriven, whose earliest comment along these lines was, I believe, around 1970.

Meta-Evaluation Criteria. This brief analysis suggests five meta-evaluation criteria for our listening and talking about AEA's evaluation policy initiative:

1. Is our thinking sufficiently considering the Big Picture?
2. Are we looking sufficiently outward?
3. Is the rising generation of evaluators leading these efforts?
4. Are we thinking specifically enough, or just in generalities?
5. Are we giving proper respect to the diversity of our field?

In Conclusion: A Story From a Time of Mixed Hope and Memory, and a Return to the Poem

The title of this chapter refers to memory and hope in evaluation policy and practice. This final section offers a story that shows that there is indeed reason to hope and concludes with the poem from which the images of golden sand and boats on rivers referred to in the title and opening paragraph are drawn.

The Story. One of the great good achievements of the past 2 years has been the reauthorization of Public Law 111–293, signed on July 30, 2008: The Tom Lantos and Henry J. Hyde United States Global Leadership against

HIV/AIDS, Tuberculosis, and Malaria Reauthorization Act of 2008. Authorized at $48 billion, this legislation represents the United States at its best in world leadership in providing assistance to foreign countries for prevention and treatment of these diseases. The Lundry Foundation of Denver has focused on evaluation. The Lundry CEO contacted our own Jody Fitzpatrick of the University of Denver for guidance on evaluation provisions. Jody connected the foundation with George Grob, leader of our AEA Policy Task Force, who worked closely with the lobbying firm Patton Boggs. The law includes a notable and complex array of evaluation initiations: monitoring, promising practices, evaluations, operations research, evaluation planning, mandated studies, and dissemination of results. The groundwork for such provisions was set, in part, by the congressionally mandated study carried out by the Institute of Medicine of the implementation of the initial legislation. As Grob discussed in our 2008 meeting, trying to improve the reauthorization evaluation provisions was a win some, lose some experience, particularly with the operations research terms. Still, it is a start. Influence is far from easy—and this is as it should be—but also far from impossible!

And the Poem
Dark brown is the river
Golden is the sand
It flows along forever
Trees on either hand.
Green leaves floating
Castles on the foam
Boats of our aboating
Where will they come home?
On down the river
A hundred miles or more
Other little children
Will bring our boats ashore.

We ourselves have brought ashore boats launched by evaluators such as Don Campbell, Peter Rossi, Marcia Guttentag, and Egon Guba. The evaluation policies we launch today will be brought ashore by evaluators now beginning their graduate studies, by those just entering college, and those even younger. I have great confidence that, working together, these policies will be not unworthy.

References

Adams, H., & Adams, B. (1919). *The degradation of the democratic dogma*. New York: Macmillan.

American Evaluation Association. (2008, March 1). Letter to Robert Shea, Office of Management and Budget.

American Evaluation Association Policy Task Force. (2007). *AEA evaluation policy task force charges,* June 2007. Retrieved June 25, 2008, from http://www.eval.org/EPTF.charge.asp

Cahalan, M. (2008, November). A PART tragedy—The case of upward bound: Correcting for study error in the national evaluation of upward bound. Paper presented at the American Evaluation Association meeting, Denver, CO.

Chelimsky, E. (2008). A clash of cultures: Improving the "fit" between evaluative independence and the political requirements of a democratic society. *American Journal of Evaluation, 29,* 400–415.

Coalition for Evidence-Based Policy. (2008). Coalition to launch initiative to identify and validate social interventions meeting "top-tier" evidence of effectiveness. Washington, DC: Council for Excellence in Government, 2008. Retrieved July 9, 2009, from http://otrans.3cdn.net/4059e8bdad5e506fde_qjm6ih0a1.pdf

Darling-Hammond, L., & Youngs, P. (2002, December). Defining "highly qualified teachers": What does "scientifically-based research" actually tell us? *Educational Researcher,* 13–25.

Emerson, R. W. (1841, December 9). The conservative. Lecture delivered at the Masonic Temple, Boston. Published in *Nature, Addresses and Lectures.*

European Evaluation Society. (2007). EES statement: The importance of a methodologically diverse approach to impact evaluation—Specifically with respect to development aid and development interventions. Netherlands: ESS Secretariat. Retrieved July 9, 2009, from http://www.europeanevaluation.org/news?newsId=1969406

Julnes, G., & Rog, D. J. (Eds.). (2007). Informing federal policies on evaluation methodology: Building the evidence base for method choice in government sponsored evaluation. *New Directions for Evaluation,* no. 113. San Francisco: Jossey-Bass.

Kagan, R. (2008). *The return of history and the end of dreams.* New York: Knopf.

Merton, R. K. (1965). *On the shoulders of giants: A Shandean postscript.* New York: Free Press.

National Center for Education Evaluation and Regional Assistance. (2003). *Identifying and implementing educational practices supported by rigorous evidence.* Retrieved October 15, 2008, from http://ies.ed.gov/ncee/pubs/evidence_based/evidence_based.asp

National Forum on Early Childhood Program Evaluation. (2007). *Early childhood program evaluations: A decision-maker's guide.* Cambridge, MA: Harvard University, Center on the Developing Child.

National Intelligence Council. (2008). *Global trends 2025: A transformed world.* Washington, DC: Author.

Overseas Development Institute (ODI). (2008). *Influence mapping.* Retrieved March 29, 2009, from http://www.odi.org.uk/rapid/Tools/Toolkits/Policy_Impact/Influence_mapping

San Francisco AIDS Foundation. (2008, July 1–8). Confronting the "evidence" in evidence-based HIV prevention: Summary report. *HIV Evidence Based Prevention.* San Francisco: Author.

Schlesinger, A. M., Jr. (1986). *Cycles of American history.* Boston: Houghton-Mifflin.

U.S. Government Printing Office. (2008). P.L. 110-293 (HR 5501), the Tom Lantos and Henry J. Hyde United States Global Leadership Against HIV/AIDS, Tuberculosis, and Malaria Reauthorization Act of 2008. Retrieved October 25, 2008, from http://frwebgate.acess.gpo.gov/cgi-bin/getdoc.ogidbname=110_cong_public_laws&docid=f:pub/293.pfd

Viadero, D. (2008a). U.S. position on research seen in flux. *Education Week.* Retrieved September 12, 2008, from http:///www.edweek.org/ew/articles/2008/03/05/26research_eph27.html?tmp=609/

Viadero, D. (2008b). Fellowships aim to nurture research talent. *Education Week*. Retrieved August 21, 2008, from http://www.edweek.org/ew/articles

White, H. (2008). Interview, International Initiative for Impact Evaluation. Center for Global Development. Retrieved July 31, 2008, from http://www.cgdev.org/content/opinion/detail/15102

Zakaria, F. (2008). *The post-American world*. New York: Norton.

LOIS-ELLIN DATTA has been national director of Head Start evaluation; director of research on teaching, learning, and assessment for the U.S. National Institute of Education; and director of program evaluation in the human service areas at the U.S. Government Accountability Office. She currently is president of Datta Analysis, consulting in the areas of policy and methodology.

Chelimsky, E. (2009). Integrating evaluation units into the political environment of government: The role of evaluation policy. In W.M.K. Trochim, M. M. Mark, & L. J. Cooksy (Eds.),
Evaluation policy and evaluation practice. New Directions for Evaluation, 123, 51–66.

4

Integrating Evaluation Units Into the Political Environment of Government: The Role of Evaluation Policy

Eleanor Chelimsky

Abstract

Most discussions of evaluation policy focus on the substance and process of doing evaluations. However, doing evaluations in government requires careful consideration not only of evaluation but also of the larger political structure into which it is expected to fit. I argue in this chapter that success for evaluation in government depends as much on the political context within which evaluation operates as it does on the merits of the evaluation process itself. For convenience, I divide the contextual governmental pressures on evaluation into three kinds: those stemming from the overarching structure of our democracy, those stemming from the bureaucratic climate of a particular agency, and those stemming from the dominant professional culture within that agency. I then examine how those three kinds of pressures have, in my experience, affected the independence, credibility, and ethical position of the evaluation units and evaluators concerned. Finally, I offer some suggestions for evaluation policy in the hope of avoiding a repetition of past evaluative failures that resulted either from unawareness of political relationships in government or from the inability of small evaluation units to protect their work in the face of much more powerful political forces. © Wiley Periodicals, Inc.

NEW DIRECTIONS FOR EVALUATION, no. 123, Fall 2009   © Wiley Periodicals, Inc., and the American Evaluation
Association.   Published online in Wiley InterScience (www.interscience.wiley.com) • DOI: 10.1002/ev.305

For some years now, I have been arguing that we take too narrow a focus when we think about evaluation policy. Normally, we have in mind improving the substance and process of doing evaluations, especially their design, implementation, and reporting. But if we want to improve the performance and success of evaluation *in government*, then we must also consider the context of the evaluation enterprise, and in particular the political environment in which evaluations are conducted. Why should we worry about this environment? Because it generates the questions that are posed to evaluation; because it drives a multitude of evaluative decisions; because it may or may not welcome the evaluative search for answers; and because it is so powerful that it can easily scatter, bend, or break those evaluative efforts that become entangled in its net.

In other words, we should not imagine that we can readily insert evaluation into the existing machinery of government. On the contrary, I would argue that some of evaluation's most resounding failures can be traced to problems of fit between even the most expert of evaluation units and its political environment. But to begin dealing with some of these problems of fit, we need a better understanding of their specifics, and a reasonable way to target our efforts into so much complexity.

One way to start might be to recognize three distinct sources, or levels, of political pressure emerging from that environment, which have posed problems in the past for evaluation units in government.

Three Levels of Political Pressure

The first level to consider is the overall "checks-and-balances" architecture of government, which produces what we might call *cross-branch politics.* This is the lofty arena in which the executive and legislative branches vie for power, engage in political partisanship, and direct ramified but well-aimed strikes on evaluative processes, outcomes, and reporting—especially reporting.

Second, at a closer level, there's the *bureaucratic climate* within the agency that houses the evaluation unit. This is a climate in which agency welfare, not public truth telling, is the primary political concern, and where evaluators may experience pressures that run the gamut from the forced embrace of bureaucratic norms and values to alteration of evaluation findings that could embarrass the agency.

At the third level, nearest to the evaluation unit, we find the *dominant professional culture* of the agency (whether it be law, science, audit, or something else). This culture tends to precipitate political clashes with the evaluation culture, sometimes because of unfamiliarity (when the unit is new), sometimes because of differences in theory or practice, but most often from a sense of rivalry or resentment.

So an evaluation unit in government is embedded as in a set of Russian dolls: first, within a branch of that government; inside that branch, within an agency; and inside that agency, within a professional culture. To be successful, the unit must integrate itself into its multilevel, often hostile political environment, but at the same time generate sound studies, preserve its integrity and credibility, develop its productivity, and maintain a stimulating workplace. How then do these three levels of political pressure affect evaluation efforts?

Let us begin with *cross-branch politics*. When the Congress calls for evaluation of a federal program, this fact alone raises hackles in the Executive Branch, regardless of the congressional oversight function. For legislative evaluators, this means that their entire study process may be caught within the resulting tug-of-war. On their side, executive evaluators, who may already feel pressure from administration and agency politics, are likely to encounter new political problems in the Congress if they present favorable evidence about an agency program. More fundamentally, cross-branch politics drives policy development in government, dominates the evaluative agenda, and shapes the kind of difficulty evaluators will confront, if and when the "wrong" findings have to be reported.

At the *bureaucratic* level, the implications for evaluation largely concern productivity and morale, although independence can be affected if the agency is unhappy with an evaluation's findings. Because the bureaucratic climate optimizes agency defense, it fosters self-protective, territorial, and secretive behavior in consequence. Bureaucrats especially detest whistleblowers, but they also frown on any kind of internal dissent, especially evaluative conclusions that ignore agency traditions or contradict past pronouncements. The tempo of communications in an agency often reflects which way the wind is blowing: adagio when the bureaucracy is in defense mode, but prestissimo when it comes to suppressing dissent.

At the *dominant professional* level, the political pressures on evaluation often spring from competition for standing or position within the agency, but they usually focus ostensibly on differences between the methods, standards, and values of one profession versus those of another. However, because the dominant professional culture sits comfortably within the bureaucracy (and may have been sitting there for a long, long time), an intimate relationship typically exists between the two. This means that the intruding evaluation unit must make two simultaneous integration efforts: adapt to the strictures of bureaucratic life, and also confront the issue of evaluation's legitimacy in the eyes of the professional culture.

James Wilson makes a useful distinction between professionals and bureaucrats within an agency. "Professionals," he writes, "are those employees who receive some significant portion of their incentives from organized groups of fellow practitioners located *outside* the agency." "A bureaucrat," on the other hand, is "someone whose occupational incentives come entirely from *within* the agency" (Wilson, 1989, p. 60). But although the incentives of these two groups differ, they can combine politically to become a formidable single adversary for a trespassing evaluation unit. Says Wilson: "Organizations

NEW DIRECTIONS FOR EVALUATION • DOI: 10.1002/ev

in which two or more cultures struggle for supremacy will experience serious conflict, as defenders of one seek to dominate representatives of the others" (p. 101).

Two other points should be kept in mind about this environment. First, all three levels can exert pressure concurrently, although not necessarily with the same outcome in view, so that an evaluation unit may suffer slings and arrows from several directions at once. Second, it never stands still. Ideas, policies, and political alliances are in constant flux and reflux, and this dynamism has ramifications for both the evaluation process and the policy use of findings. Heraclitus said that we can never step twice into the same river. Neither will evaluators find the same political environment at the end of a study as the one that prevailed when it began.

To summarize, I am arguing here that the political environment surrounding an evaluation unit can be usefully considered as containing three distinct sources or levels of political pressure; that this environment, in all its intricacy, is also highly mobile, especially at the cross-branch level; and that this combination of complexity and dynamism can pose severe challenges to a new evaluation unit. Therefore, conciliating the political environment that evaluation units must both confront and integrate is an essential goal for evaluation policy, which has until now concerned itself mostly with evaluation processes rather than context. But if we accept this logic, the next question has to be: How then, in such a complicated environment, can we choose effective points of entry?

Three Evaluative Requirements

I would propose that we examine those places in our collective experience where political pressures have negatively affected important evaluative requirements. If I begin with my own experience, looking back over more than thirty years of conducting studies in or for government, three of these requirements stand out as most often constrained by political pressures from any or all of the three levels: for independence, for credibility, and for a workplace consistent with high evaluator morale. Let me explain what I mean by these requirements, recognizing, of course, that this list is hardly definitive and may need to be expanded, based on the experience of others.

Evaluative Independence. The issue of independence arises because evaluators need protection against partisan influence, which can emanate from almost anywhere in government. Political pressures can affect the evaluation process at almost any phase of the study, but most importantly in two places: at the design stage (e.g., efforts to interfere with a strong design, or impose an inappropriate one) and at the final stage (e.g., efforts to influence findings and report language, or efforts to prevent publication). Political pressures on evaluators can distort what Philip Kitcher calls the "two most important contexts of decision: the formulation of projects for inquiry, and the appraisal of evidence for conclusions" (Kitcher, cited in Judson, 2004).

Thus evaluators need freedom to plan and implement the particular study design that will bring the best answer to the question asked, and they need freedom to determine their findings and report on what they've found. However, it's also the case that independence can never be an absolute value for evaluators because of their *other* need to promote the fit of their unit within the agency. Too much stiff-necked resistance will weaken a unit's chances of survival, especially in its first years. On the other hand, if evaluators succumb too often to political pressures, their unit's integrity—and *reputation* for integrity—will suffer. This brings us to the second evaluation requirement often affected by partisan influence, credibility.

Evaluative Credibility. The principal component of credibility for an evaluation unit is, of course, high-quality evaluation, and AEA's work in evaluation policy is already focusing on that. But a unit's reputation can be tarnished in ways that have little to do with actual quality or expertise: through bureaucratic or professional resentment or misunderstanding of the evaluative enterprise, for example; through agency restrictions on evaluation budgets or study topics; or through purposeful attempts to disparage or discredit evaluation reports. This again speaks to the problem of improving the fit of an evaluation unit within its agency because of the tensions involved between trying to reduce turf battles whenever possible and at the same time carefully and consistently protecting both the unit's ability to do its work and its reputation for integrity. André Malraux once said, "You don't inherit culture, you conquer it." So it is with credibility. It's not conferred; you fight for it, one evaluation at a time.

Evaluator Morale. A third requirement frequently affected by political pressure is evaluator morale. Evaluators need a place to work where they feel at least relatively free, where intellectual curiosity is tolerated, and where they're rewarded explicitly for the quality of their work. The difficulty here is that agencies tend to reward reliability over brilliance, and managerial know-how over methodological know-how. What counts most in a bureaucracy is control, fidelity to the past, loyalty to the agency. Bonuses rarely go to innovators. This, of course, is a lot closer to the Roman ideal (faithful Aeneas, pietas and gravitas, etc.) than it is to the Greek irreverence dear to evaluators: that is, questioning received wisdom, dissenting when necessary (and especially when not necessary), and acquiring inconvenient new knowledge. The mismatch here is a real one, and it regularly produces high-decibel gnashing of evaluators' teeth.

On the other hand, bureaucrats and professionals have their own teeth-gnashing problems with evaluators. At the Government Accountability Office, or GAO, where I worked for many years, we evaluators discovered by means of a survey that agency managers and staff there looked down on evaluators as "displaced academics who chafe painfully at agency rules and regulations, and may not see the need to acquire GAO skills, understand GAO values, or fulfill GAO job requirements" (USGAO/PEMD, 1990). At OMB, budget examiners expressed similar sentiments, and we found the same issue at other agencies as well. In short, there exist problems of fit within agencies, on both sides of the ledger—problems that evaluation units, unaided, may not always be able to resolve.

The IPE Experience

I turn now from the general to the particular. Because it is important to understand an agency's individual political context when trying to integrate a new unit there, I want to sketch briefly the political environment for evaluation at GAO when I went there in 1980 to start a unit that began as the Institute for Program Evaluation (or IPE) and later became GAO's Program Evaluation and Methodology Division (or PEMD). Then I illustrate, with some evaluations performed at GAO, how the tensions between politics and evaluation (described above) played out in practice. First, here is some background about the GAO context.

I remember that on my first day at GAO, no one I talked with, at either staff or management level, appeared to have a precise idea about what they expected from the Institute. It seemed that the fact of IPE's creation was more important to people than what the unit would actually do. We did have a charter in which it was stated that we would perform evaluations and also work to increase the spread of evaluative capabilities throughout the Office, but what we would do and how we would do it were left unspecified. So I spent a few weeks interviewing quite a large number of evaluation users, producers, and observers in both branches of government to get a set of educated judgments about what *they* thought we should do, and I came rapidly to the conclusion that the climate was not going to be propitious for evaluation at GAO. There were three reasons for this.

First, IPE was established as a response to severe criticism of GAO's earlier evaluative work. The issues raised had focused mostly on methodological weaknesses such as narrowness of approach, unsophisticated methods, improper generalizations, and findings that used "auditor judgment" as a substitute for data support (Singer, 1979; Bethell, 1980; Klimschot, 1980). The most general complaint was that what GAO presented as "evaluation" was really "audit." Said one critic: "These evaluations reflect the GAO's past and do not follow the procedures that social scientists use in the conduct of program evaluation" (Walker, 1985, p. 280). Indeed, during my interviews with GAO managers and staff, it became clear they did believe that audit and evaluation were the same thing, felt that the criticism of their work was therefore unwarranted, and resented not only the critics but also those Johnny-come-latelies at IPE, brought in to GAO to solve a nonexistent problem.

A second cause for worry had to do with overt in-fighting between GAO's auditors and pre-IPE evaluators. These battles had actually provoked an official comment from a House Committee in 1978:

GAO has not yet succeeded in reaching a desirable objective: the effective integration of accounting skills and techniques associated with its older functions, with the evaluative and analytical tools of the policy sciences required by its post-1970 responsibilities. Internal rivalries and competition between personnel representing the two sets of attitudes and experience continue to plague the agency and to deny to the Congress the full realization of GAO's potential.   (House Select Committee on Congressional Operations, 1978, p. viii)

The third reason for apprehension came from the literature. Anthony Downs, for example, whose bureaucratic experience as a Rand Corporation analyst is second to none, tells terrible tales about the survival difficulties of new units within agencies; he counsels them to muster support *outside* their agency if they're to resist what he calls "annihilation" from within. He especially incriminates "functional rivals"—that is, other units in an agency whose functions are similar to, or competitive with, those of the new unit. Downs writes that if a new unit has the misfortune to possess such rivals (and this was surely the case for IPE vis-à-vis the audit divisions at GAO), then "these antagonists will often seek to capture the new unit's functions themselves, or suppress them altogether"; "they will try to block it from establishing a strong external power base"; the new unit "will be severely opposed from the start"; and "the possibility that it will be destroyed by its enemies is a real one" (Downs, 1966, pp. 9, 10, 71, and 195, respectively).

In point of fact, my talks with GAO managers and staff had confirmed that IPE was not seen as a very useful addition to agency capabilities, and that efforts to eliminate it might well be in the cards. On the other hand, staff and managers from executive and legislative agencies *outside GAO* expressed belief in the reality and importance of the evaluative issues IPE was intended to address, and they brought up a host of new methodological problems for us to deal with. From members of Congress, I got pats on the head, assurances of support, and some quite useful information about what various committees were hoping for from IPE.

It is probably fair to say that the difficulties we encountered as a new evaluation unit were pretty much what the agency context and the literature would have led you to expect. Naturally, I moved quickly to establish a strong relationship with congressional committees, developing a ten-pronged strategy for improving GAO's evaluation capabilities (Chelimsky, 1990). Just as naturally, some parts of the strategy worked, some didn't, and some efforts that weren't even part of the strategy but arose spontaneously worked best of all. Still, IPE was not "annihilated," although some certainly tried to do so; instead, we actually flourished, the work was exciting, and many of us received awards, bonuses, and promotions. As for me, I went to GAO in 1980 believing with Santayana that if you ignore history, you'll be condemned to repeat it. I left there in 1994, believing with Heine that what we learn from history is that we do *not* learn from history. (Both were right, of course, but one of them thought normatively, the other descriptively.)

This, then, gives an idea of where things stood at GAO when IPE began. Over time, we would grasp that the pressures brought by cross-branch, bureaucratic, and professional cultures are real, frequent, and often damaging. Most of the nearly 300 evaluations we eventually conducted at GAO reflect some kind of intervention from these three political sources, singly or in combination, as I now illustrate.

Effects of Political Pressures on Three Evaluative Requirements

How the three political pressures actually constrained our work at GAO can be examined by looking at their operation as they collided with individual evaluative requirements during the performance of three particular studies. Let me start with pressures on independence.

Evaluative Independence. At GAO, independence is protected both by statute and by tradition. An essential aim of GAO's enabling legislation (Budget and Accounting Act of 1921) was "to limit the extent to which the agency would be subject to partisan political pressures from either the Executive Branch or the Congress" (Murphy, 1994, p. 1). IPE, and later PEMD, benefited greatly from this protection, which was hugely effective where pressures external to GAO were concerned. This is not to say that political pressures were never exerted on IPE, but rather that, when evaluative independence is a value accepted by all parties involved, it is much easier to defend.

Consider, for example, an evaluation we were doing in PEMD, looking at the relationship between car size and safety. The Senate Committee on Commerce, Science, and Transportation had introduced fuel-efficiency legislation in early 1990 requiring that automobiles get 34 miles per gallon of gas by the year 1996, instead of the current 27. One aim of the bill was to save an estimated 2.5 million barrels of oil *per day*. The auto industry had issued a statement warning that if the bill passed, the consequent downsizing of American autos would produce a fleet of dangerously unsafe small cars certain to "increase the number of deaths and injuries on U.S. highways" (NHTSA, 1991, p. 37). So the committee asked us to examine the basis for believing that smaller cars are less safe than larger ones. Our evaluation made use of the Fatal Accident Reporting System data file, merged with registration data, along with state police accident reports.

In April 1991, I testified on our progress to date and told the committee that: "Heavier cars are not invariably safer than lighter ones; indeed, the highest fatality rates are in cars in the middle of the weight distribution. When two cars of different masses collide, of course, the smaller *is* likely to sustain more damage than the larger one. However, we estimate that if the proportion of small cars on the road were to grow substantially, the total fatality rate in two-car accidents would decline, due to the decreased likelihood of comparatively deadly collisions between large and small cars." In short, we said it was "not true that cars become more dangerous simply by getting lighter" (Chelimsky, 1991).

A few days after this testimony, I received the first in a series of unhappy letters from Congressman John Dingell of Michigan, a Democrat who opposed the legislation. As the *New York Times* reported in 1991: "By his own account, Mr. Dingell is the automobile industry's chief spokesman in Congress. He has devoted himself to blocking automobile safety, fuel economy requirements, and anti-pollution legislation. 'I am totally unapologetic about that,' he said. 'I represent half a million people whose lives are controlled by the good fortune or bad fortune of the auto industry. I was sent down here to look after the welfare of that district and the people I serve'" (Rosenbaum, 1991, S1-p.1). Obviously, our assessment of the auto industry's position did not sit well with Congressman Dingell.

Over a period of 7 months, he sent us letters questioning our work, our expertise, and our motives, and asking us for so much more research that he kept us busy far into the night just to answer him and also keep abreast of the committee's evaluation. But despite our efforts, he finally sent us a letter putting into question our ability to publish our work. It was this potential interference with the publication of a GAO report that triggered an immediate response from GAO's deputy comptroller general, who arranged for a formal meeting with the congressman's chief of staff to resolve the issues. Together the DCG and I went up to the Hill for what turned out to be an amazingly low-key encounter. Nothing whatever was said about independence, but it was, of course, the gorilla in the room. We reached an agreement that we would continue the work we'd planned to do anyway; that we would conduct some new research for Mr.Dingell; that we would keep the congressman advised as our work progressed; and finally, that we would send him copies of our publications, when—not if—they were issued.

That was the end of the problem. We published without incident and actually went on to do a number of evaluations for Mr. Dingell.

Over the years, our independence was very well defended against partisan influence from outside GAO, and this shows that such protection is feasible for evaluators working within a political environment. But we were not so lucky when it came to attacks by "functional rivals" within GAO. However, these agency storms tended to leave our independence more or less intact if we fought hard enough for it. Instead, their major impact was on productivity, morale, and especially our reputation for expertise, our credibility.

Evaluative Credibility. Perhaps no study we did at GAO better illustrates the effect on a new evaluation unit of losing credibility than does our early evaluation of the AFDC program (Aid to Families with Dependent Children). It began with a phone call from a staff member at the House

Ways and Means Committee in early October 1981, asking us to evaluate the effects of recent changes to the AFDC program. Some of you may recall this period: President Reagan had been elected in 1980, Charles Murray was writing *Losing Ground*, and welfare policy had taken a sharp right turn, complete with clever little twists of language—the "social insurance" of Franklin Roosevelt's day was now called "welfare dependency," and as Moynihan put it, "What was once seen as charity is now redefined as cruelty" (Moynihan, 1996, p. 33). To conservatives, of course, the change was welcome, part of a needed effort to move people from welfare to work.

Now, in the summer of 1981, the Congress, following the Reagan administration's lead, had passed legislation known as OBRA (the Omnibus Budget Reconciliation Act) and the October phone call from Ways and Means reflected the Republican-Democratic split on welfare policy. OBRA had included more than 20 changes to AFDC provisions, virtually all of them oriented toward cuts of various types in the program. Republicans on the committee were interested in OBRA's effects on overall welfare costs and caseloads, while Democrats wanted to know about OBRA's effects on family or household composition and, for those families removed from the program, effects on earning patterns and economic well-being.

It was evident that IPE would need a greatly increased budget to take on a national evaluation of the size suggested by the committee. Accordingly, I had to refer their question to GAO's top management, which opened the Ways and Means request to discussion and debate across GAO. Staff from one of IPE's functional rival divisions argued that the job should be theirs because they had audited welfare programs in the past, and they contacted the committee to take over the proposed work. But when the auditors explained their ideas for the evaluation, the committee staff made clear that what they wanted was a cause-and-effect study, not the compliance review the auditors were suggesting, and that this was why they had approached IPE in the first place.

The auditors then told Ways and Means that IPE had been established at GAO uniquely to assist the audit divisions in their work, and that it had neither the authorization nor the capability to perform program evaluations. This was, of course, absurd, given the IPE charter and expertise, but it had the effect of confusing the Hill staffers, and it set in motion a long chain of committee-induced meetings at GAO, featuring agreements and dissent, dueling position papers, feints, rebuttals, maneuvers, and complaints. This period ended when GAO assigned the study to the *audit* division in June 1982, some eight months after the original phone call to me. The assignment was, however, contingent on committee approval of the auditors' evaluation design.

When the committee rejected that design, GAO then gave IPE the responsibility for developing a new design, but *only* the design; implementation, management, and operational control of the evaluation would remain with the audit division. Although this arrangement seemed a little short on feasibility, we tried to be good soldiers and went ahead with the design until the constant disagreements with the auditors drove me, in November, to renegotiate IPE's participation in the evaluation. At this point, the auditors bowed out, the study was reassigned to IPE, and by December 1982 we were finally able to present a completed evaluation design to Ways and Means.

In sum, more than a year had been spent on rivalry and in-fighting, our workplace had become a sort of fortress, resentment ran high against us in the audit division, and from the viewpoint of fitting in this was no victory, not even Pyrrhic. Worse, our reputation on the Hill was in shreds, and this could have seriously undermined not only the acceptance of our eventual findings on the AFDC evaluation but also IPE's overall strategy for gaining external support in the Congress. In practical terms, the loss of credibility we sustained forced us to accept an almost unmanageable set of "coordination" hurdles throughout the evaluation: coordination with the audit division on even the most minor points, coordination with multiple advisory boards, and coordination with a number of committee-stipulated organizations outside GAO.

We did regain credibility over time, and the Congress used our findings well, passing new legislation that restored health benefits to working families forced by OBRA to leave AFDC. This wasn't a bad result, when you consider the war raging on welfare policy, along with the efforts to discredit our work. However, the damage here could have been irreparable, and from an evaluation policy perspective the lesson is that attacks on a new evaluation unit's credibility do happen, and the younger and less entrenched the unit, the more dangerous they're likely to be.

Evaluator Morale. As mentioned earlier, one challenge that evaluators face in trying to integrate their political environment comes from the tension between *their* training and perspectives and those of other agency staff. But among the many tension-based issues that concern us here, perhaps none looms as large, both for evaluation policy and for evaluators, as does the clash between loyalty to one's agency and allegiance to evaluative norms and standards. This problem befell us in PEMD, with respect to an evaluation conducted by another GAO division. The question they were answering was whether the Immigration Reform and Control Act (known as IRCA) had caused employment discrimination to increase in the U.S. workplace.

Recall that the IRCA legislation was enacted in 1986, after many years of public battling among a variety of interest groups involved in issues such as the enforcement of U.S. labor laws, the number of undocumented people crossing U.S. borders, and the labor-market problems of employers in sectors of the U.S. economy where workers are in short supply. The new law sought to establish the legal status of workers as an employment standard, and to achieve this it imposed sanctions (i.e., civil and criminal penalties) on employers who hired undocumented workers. There was, however, some concern that the sanctions could lead to unintentional discrimination against *legal* workers by employers nervous about making a mistake. To deal

NEW DIRECTIONS FOR EVALUATION • DOI: 10.1002/ev

with this concern, a special feature was incorporated into the law: the GAO would conduct an evaluation to determine whether there was indeed more discrimination after IRCA than before, and if so, whether the increase could be directly attributed to the IRCA sanctions. If the GAO concluded that they had in fact increased discrimination, then the Congress could repeal them quickly via expedited procedures contained in the law.

In March 1990, then, the GAO report—on time and in final draft, but not yet published—was ready to be delivered to the Hill when letters began arriving at GAO alleging that the study's "flawed methodology" was inadequate to support its conclusions. It was at this point that I was summoned and asked to take a look at the problem. I had never heard of the study before because, at GAO, coordination was a responsibility only for IPE. (We told the audit divisions regularly what we were doing, but they were not required to discuss their work with us and didn't do so). I remember that it was a Friday afternoon, and I was asked to produce a review of the study's methodology by Monday. I realized, of course, that the review was expected to be favorable. I went home for the weekend with five briefcases, methodological angst, and a migraine.

The news was not good. The GAO report concluded that the IRCA sanctions had indeed increased employment discrimination, but it presented only fragile evidence for this cause-and-effect relationship. Because no baseline data had been developed in 1986 when the act was passed, there were no before-and-after comparisons of employment discrimination, and the design used a single, after-only survey of employers. So the conclusion of an IRCA-caused increase reposed entirely on one item in the survey that measured employer recall about pre-IRCA behavior. This meant there were two problems: using a single-shot survey to establish causality, and assuming the validity and reliability of recall, which is almost never a strong measure. In this case, it was especially weak because there were neither backup data nor records to rely on for support. The study team *had* looked for indications of increase in other publicly available data sets, but some of them actually pointed in the opposite direction. That is, there was no difference in the rates at which Hispanics and other minorities got jobs pre- and post-IRCA, and no increase in national-origin charges of discrimination filed with EEOC after IRCA.

I wrote my review over the weekend, worded it carefully, recommended changes in the report's language, along with a bold retreat from its conclusions, and delivered it on Monday, but with little or no result. The authors of the report made only small modifications to their draft, tinkering a bit with a few things (the title, for example, was changed appropriately). However, the claim of increased discrimination due to the IRCA sanctions was maintained, despite my efforts.

At this point, I went off on annual leave, the GAO report was released (USGAO/GGD, 1990), and it was immediately followed by introduction of legislation to repeal the IRCA sanctions, based on the GAO findings. Yet only a few weeks later, I returned from vacation to discover that my review had been leaked, printed in its entirety—together with passionate commentary by a U.S. senator—in the Congressional Record (Congressional Record-Senate, 1990) and used to discredit the GAO report. The end result was that the Congress did *not* act to repeal the sanctions, and PEMD became, for a time, a very difficult place in which to work.

In my judgment, this case is an important one for evaluation policy. Although no one could (or did, to my knowledge) claim that the GAO report constituted strong evaluation, the issue here was not about good research, or about being right, but about politics. The auditors were defending their judgment and "standing by their report." For the bureaucrats, it was "my agency right or wrong," combined with an opportunity to suppress internal dissent. For GAO's top management, the choice was between looking stupid momentarily, perhaps, and losing power and credibility over the long run if they *didn't* stand by their report. For cross-branch politicians, my review was just another political tool in the Republican-Democratic battle over immigration reform.

The problem for *evaluators* is, once again, balancing professional standards and norms with fitting in. The problem for evaluation *policy* is how to protect evaluators from this kind of situation in which trilevel politics will always trump research.

Six Suggestions for Evaluation Policy

In conclusion, I offer a set of suggestions as to how those concerned about evaluation policy can help deal with the political pressures and resulting challenges that I have described. It goes without saying that not all new evaluation units necessarily have the benefits with respect to independence or face problems of the same intensity that IPE confronted at GAO. There are a number of reasons for this. Legislative agencies are not the same as executive agencies; executive and legislative agencies, as well as evaluation units, differ among themselves; contexts for introducing an evaluation unit into an agency are variable; some dominant professional cultures may be less competitive with evaluation than auditing; not all evaluation units are charged with spreading evaluative capabilities throughout an agency; and the year 2010 is not 1980. But the sources or levels of political pressure are identical, the pressures themselves notably increased during the second Bush administration, especially where independence was concerned, and the places in our evaluation processes where we are most likely to chafe under those pressures have not changed. So the experience is utterly relevant, and I draw from it six points that I hope will be helpful in our future thinking about evaluation policy.

First, we need strong, current information about problems and successes that evaluators are experiencing in their workplaces, and about which parts of the evaluation process are being affected by what political

NEW DIRECTIONS FOR EVALUATION • DOI: 10.1002/ev

pressures. To target evaluation policy efforts reasonably well, and avoid being overtaken by events, it might be a good idea to schedule sessions with evaluators, on a regular, ongoing basis, to discuss difficulties they may be having with respect to the design, conduct, and reporting of their work, along with questions of ethics, independence, credibility, and general workplace issues.

Second, agency history is of great significance for evaluative integration, and every agency is different. It might be useful if evaluation policy could emphasize, especially for new units, the importance of understanding their agency's experience (e.g., professional skill areas, culture, recent political battles, historical values and their evolution, rules and regulations, and so forth). This can be crucial in avoiding unnecessary strife with bureaucratic colleagues.

Third, evaluation policy needs to consider ways and means for evaluation units to conciliate the dominant professional culture in their agency. Here it may be wise to think about tactics that include outreach, defense, and deterrence. With respect to outreach, for example, we evaluators at GAO made a continuing effort at dialogue and collaboration, familiarizing ourselves with auditing and accounting methods. At other agencies, evaluators have absorbed principles of engineering, environmental science, budget examination, and law, to mention only a few. With respect to defensive tactics, evaluation policy should recognize the value of an expert advisory board in ensuring a unit's legitimacy, both within the agency and beyond it, as well as in protecting its study processes. As for deterrence, a useful tactic would be to increase awareness among top agency officials of the functional-rival problem and seek to involve those officials directly in its mitigation. That is, if everyone in an agency knew that public attacks on a new evaluation unit would not be rewarded and might even be sanctioned, this could be very helpful in heading them off.

Fourth, the principle of evaluative independence is worth fighting for. Evaluation policy should seek to gain wider acceptance in government for its protection. Whether partisan pressures are applied from inside or outside the agency, whether they're exercised on study findings or study designs, and whether they're disguised or overt, they need to be countered if evaluation units are to do their job. At GAO, the existing protections of evaluative and audit independence against external political pressures are of such great benefit that they should be extended, where possible, to executive branch evaluation units, which have often been poorly protected against cross-branch political interference.

Fifth, the conflict between loyalty to one's agency and conformity with evaluation principles can be a deal breaker for evaluators and their units. Evaluation policy needs to consider a strategy for handling such problems, including, for example, a provision for inviting external evaluation experts to substitute for the unit in cases where this type of conflict is likely to arise.

NEW DIRECTIONS FOR EVALUATION • DOI: 10.1002/ev

Finally, it is helpful for evaluators entering government service to understand how bureaucracies work. If these evaluators are familiar with the cultural values and complexity of the political environment that they'll need to accommodate, then it will cost them less, in terms of time and stomach lining, to make a reasonable adjustment; it will be easier for them to negotiate successful outcomes, and they'll prepare more effectively to defend their evaluative choices. This might be facilitated both in evaluator training programs at universities and also perhaps in AEA sessions on evaluation policy.

Of course, we should not be overoptimistic about our chances of achieving a glovelike fit between evaluation units and the political environment of government. After all, evaluation exists to report on government, not be a part of it. Also, some elements of cross-branch politics will always be outside our control. As Charles Beard once said, "Politics is the art of looking for trouble, finding it everywhere, diagnosing it wrong, and applying unsuitable remedies." I don't expect evaluation policy to change that; nor is it likely that programs or policies that are rushed through in times of political crisis can be slowed long enough to permit evaluation policy intervention in the shape of accountability provisions or even a reasonable evaluation design. But what evaluation policy *can* do is look honestly and systematically at the political pressures evaluators face in government workplaces, and do what can be done both to spread understanding of these pressures and to avoid or reduce their effects.

References

Bethell, T. N. (1980). The best job in Washington. *Washington Monthly, 12*(2), 12–22.

Chelimsky, E. (1990). Expanding GAO's capabilities in program evaluation. *GAO Journal, 8*, 43–52.

Chelimsky, E. (1991, April 11). Automobile weight and safety. (Testimony before the Senate Committee on Commerce, Science and Transportation.) USGAO/T-PEMD-91-2, pp. 1 and 13.

Congressional Record. (1990, July 17). GAO's finding of discrimination based on employer sanctions, Senate, pp. S9806–S9808.

Downs, A. (1966). *Inside bureaucracy* (pp. 9, 10, 71, 195). New York: Little, Brown.

House Select Committee on Congressional Operations. (1978, June 22). *General Accounting Office services to the Congress: An assessment.* Washington, DC: USGPO.

Judson, H. F. (2004). *The great betrayal: Fraud in science.* Orlando, FL: Harcourt, Brace.

Klimschot, J. (1980). *Adding bite to the bark: A Common Cause study of the GAO, the government's watchdog.* Washington, DC: Common Cause.

Moynihan, D. P. (1996, January 11). Congress builds a coffin. *New York Times Review of Books,* p. 33.

Murphy, R. P. (1994, February 3). On GAO independence. *USGAO,* p. 1.

National Highway Traffic Safety Administration (NHTSA). (1991, April). *Small car/large car crash tests.* Washington, DC: Author.

Rosenbaum, D. E. (1991, September 30). Michigan Democrat presides as Capital's grand inquisitor. *New York Times,* S1-p.1. Retrieved July 9, 2009, from http://www.nytimes.com/1991/09/30/us/washington-at-work-michigan-democrat-presides-as-capital-s-grand-inquisitor.html

Singer, J. W. (1979, November 10). When the evaluators are evaluated, the GAO often gets low marks. *National Journal*, pp. 1889–1892.

USGAO/GGD-90-62. (1990, March). *Immigration reform: Employer sanctions and the question of discrimination.* Washington, DC: United States Government Printing Office.

USGAO/PEMD-90–18. (1990, April). *Diversifying and expanding technical skills at GAO* (pp. 21, 23). Washington, DC: United States Government Printing Office.

Walker, W. E. (1985). The conduct of program evaluation reviews in the GAO. *Evaluation and Program Planning, 8,* 272–280.

Wilson, J. Q. (1989). *Bureaucracy.* New York: Basic Books.

ELEANOR CHELIMSKY *is currently a consultant in evaluation policy and practice. She was Assistant Comptroller General of the U.S. Government Accountability Office for Evaluation and Methodology, and for 14 years, ran a division at GAO of about 100 social scientists who performed evaluations for the Congress in a variety of subject areas (e.g., health, the environment defense, energy, transportation, agriculture, education, welfare, and so forth). She was a Fulbright Scholar in Paris, France, an economic and statistical analyst at NATO, and has been president of both the Evaluation Research Society and the American Evaluation Association. In 1991, she received the GAO's top honor, the Comptroller General's Award for Excellence.*

NEW DIRECTIONS FOR EVALUATION • DOI: 10.1002/ev

Stern, E. (2009). Evaluation policy in the European Union and its institutions. In W.M.K. Trochim, M. M. Mark, & L. J. Cooksy (Eds.), *Evaluation policy and evaluation practice. New Directions for Evaluation, 123*, 67–85.

Evaluation Policy in the European Union and Its Institutions

Elliot Stern

Abstract

The European Union (EU), with 27 member states, has been a significant promoter of evaluation in Europe. More than a decade of reform and modernization of EU institutions underpins the expansion of evaluation and has shaped evaluation policies. Links between evaluation uptake and policy on the one hand and public management and institutional reform on the other are highlighted. However, it is argued that the emergence of new policy instruments, new substantive policy goals, and institutional dynamics underpinned by competing narratives of the European "project," help explain how evaluation policy has evolved. The chapter considers how EU evaluation impinges on EU member states. © Wiley Periodicals, Inc.

In this chapter, I discuss the specific ways in which European and EU evaluation policy has evolved. These specificities derive mainly from the nature of the European Union (EU), the broader European "project" to build the Union, and the reform process that has been an EU institutional leitmotiv over the last decade. To generalize to any degree about European experience is of course dangerous. Across the 27 countries that now make

up the EU, history, institutions, culture, government, and civil society are extremely varied. Scholars have debated how these variations are translated into public management and governance, which inevitably also sets a frame for evaluation policy (Pollitt & Bouckaert, 2004; Rosamond, 2000; Furubo, Rist, & Sandahl, 2002; Hayward & Menon, 2003). Although there are common EU evaluation drivers, many of them coming from EU institutions based in Brussels, the context and response in different countries is distinctive and necessarily contingent on national circumstance and histories. This chapter focuses on evaluation by EU institutions: the European Commission, the executive arm of the EU which acts as guardian of EU treaties and also has powers of policy initiation; the Council of the EU, through which member state ministers represent their governments; and the European Parliament, an assembly directly elected by EU citizens since 1979.[1]

The Spread of Evaluation in Europe

Jan-Eric Furubo and colleagues (Furubo et al., 2002), in their *International Atlas of Evaluation,* reviewed evaluation experience in 21 countries and three international organizations, including the EU. In particular, they considered the internal and external pressures to take up evaluation in numerous countries. The *Atlas* acknowledges the extent to which the EU was one important external pressure for expansion of evaluation among European countries. Wollman and associates (2003) also attempted to understand the spread of evaluation in 16 countries, including a number of European states. Wollman directly links the emergence and shaping of evaluation with public sector reform. He posits three waves in evaluation development. The first, in the 1960s and 1970s, was associated with "proactive policy making" in advanced (and at that time expanding) welfare states.[2] The second wave began in the mid-1970s following the oil price shock and was "dominated by the need for budgetary retrenchment and cost efficiency" (Wollman, 2003, p. 2). The third wave, beginning in the late eighties, was associated with various forms of the New Public Management and internalization of evaluative practices within the public sector.

Furubo et al. (2002) and Wollman (2003) represent two starting assumptions: that the EU has been an important driver for diffusion of evaluation practice in Europe, and that public sector reform is one of the internal drivers for evaluation uptake and consolidation. These (and other) international comparisons of evaluation focus on central government and public management, where evaluation essentially supports decision making and enables accountability. They tend to underplay the volume and diversity of evaluative activity in decentralized settings, such as schools, neighborhoods, health centers, and commercial companies. Given that this chapter is primarily concerned with evaluation as promoted by the EU institutionally and in particular by the European Commission, starting from a central government perspective is reasonable. But as discussed below, tracing the EU's influence on evaluation within member states gives a partial picture of evaluation within specific countries.

Scale and Scope of EU Evaluation

The Commission undertook 203 evaluations in 2007, and this work was overwhelmingly contracted out to external evaluators (European Commission, hereafter EC in citations, Multi-annual, 2008a; Statistical, 2008; see References). Well over a thousand evaluations were conducted between 2000 and 2007, with a build-up over time. In 1996, 45 evaluations were commissioned, compared to 80 in 2000, 170 in 2005, and 203 in 2007. According to the European Court of Auditors, annual expenditure on evaluation amounts to approximately €45 million. However, these figures reflect only evaluations directly initiated by the Commission and do not include the many hundreds of evaluations initiated every year by member states in policy areas funded through European budgets. For example, in 2008 112 Structural Fund and Cohesion Policy evaluations were undertaken in Poland alone (Bienias, 2009).

Although most evaluations are retrospective (ex post in EU parlance), there have been an increasing number of prospective evaluations because of the commitment to "Impact Assessments," as that method is defined as part of EU management reforms in recent years. Evaluations run the full gamut of EU policy domains, including education, research, regional policy, telecommunications, external relations, health, employment, and justice.

The editors of the *International Atlas of Evaluation* recognize that the genesis of evaluation in North America was associated with education and social welfare programs. There is a similar sectoral dimension to evaluation in the European Union. Even though evaluation now permeates most EU activities and directorates general (an administrative unit roughly equivalent to government ministries), evaluation has had the greatest influence at the member-state level and in particular where European competence (powers and mandate) is strongest. The main entry point for evaluation in countries joining the Union is through Structural Funds (European Regional Development Fund, European Social Fund, and Cohesion Fund) and Cohesion Policy.[3] The well-articulated evaluation system associated with these policies has been continuously elaborated since 1988. It now places the obligation for ex ante evaluation (appraisal at the planning stage) and midterm evaluations on national authorities.

Attempting to fulfill these obligations, especially in the early years of EU membership, brings home to national authorities the importance of evaluation capacity. The responsible directorates general (REGIO, EMPLOY, and ENLARGE) have supported evaluation capacity development in various ways: through transition funding before and soon after EU accession, explicitly targeted at capacity development including training of evaluators; by sponsoring "twinning arrangements" between experts in evaluation (among other specialties) from established member states and their opposite numbers among the new members; by organizing evaluation network meetings in Brussels, nationally or at the regional level; and by providing guidance material and advice, including a series of guides to evaluation thinking and practice. (The latest of these, the EVALSED GUIDE, 2007, is available online.[4])

Evaluation Policy in Brussels

There is no single document that summarizes EU evaluation policies in Brussels. EU evaluation activity and hence evaluation policy is mainly located in the Commission rather than in the other EU institutions. Evaluation from the Commission's perspective is largely intended to support its own decision making and strategies, which has given rise to some unease in other European institutions. The chair of the European Parliament's Committee on Budgetary Control argues that Parliament should therefore initiate its own evaluations: "A parliamentary evaluation function would try to make transparent to the citizens what they are getting for their money. This objective is quite different from predominantly helping the policy system to justify how it is spending the money. Evaluation should not be brought down to a 'management tool' as is now the case in the EU system" (Bosch, 2008). These rumblings of discontent signal a conceptual cleavage in EU evaluation discourse—one of use and usefulness, of public management and efficiency—that is rarely challenged.

Legal and Political Basis. The legal basis for European Commission evaluations is enshrined in the EU's Financial Regulations, which specify the scope, purpose, timing, and use of evaluations (see Article 27, EC Financial Regulation, 2008). In addition, there are sector-specific regulations, for example in relation to Structural Funds and Research.

The Financial Regulations set a minimum level of evaluative activity that has been considerably extended by a series of Communications—policy statements by European Commissioners with responsibility for evaluation-related policies (EC SEC 96/659, 1996; EC SEC 1051, 2000; EC COM 276, 2002; EC SEC 213, 2007). The 1996 Communication on Evaluation required that all Directorates General had their own evaluation functions or units; the 2000 Communication was "concerned with the planning and implementation of evaluation activities by the Commission for its own decision making purposes" and highlighted links with results-based management; the 2002 Communication focused on Impact Assessment, the ex ante regulatory and planning tool at early stages of policy planning; and the 2007 *Communication Responding to Strategic Needs: Reinforcing the Use of Evaluation* had as its main objectives integration of evaluation at a strategic level and strengthening links with policy making.

What Is to Be Evaluated? The 1996 Communication required that "actions financed on an annual basis should be evaluated at least once every six years; multi-annual programs should be subject to midterm and ex post evaluations; and evaluation reports are to be made available well before the adoption of proposals they are meant to influence." There is also an assumption that spending on evaluation should in some way be proportionate to the actions concerned. Evaluative activity prior to 2000 focused on expenditure programs, but since the 2000 Communication, evaluation now extends to all the major activities of the Commission including legislation, soft law, networking, and internal services.

What Forms of Evaluation Are Undertaken? Since 2002, integration of evaluation and decision making specifically links evaluation to the decision-making cycle. Ex ante evaluation aids planning and programming; interim evaluation is partly for accountability but also assists program and policy managements' midterm; and ex post evaluations combine accountability, lesson learning, and sometimes causal analyses. There are also many other evaluation variants, among them thematic and synthesis reviews, real-time evaluations, and forms of action research that support program actors' innovation and learning.

Certain methodological approaches are recommended and expected if not mandated. For example, the Commission is committed to analyzing "intervention logics," defined as "a set of hypothetical cause and effect linkages that describe how an intervention is expected to attain its global objectives." These can range from relatively simple logic models to much more complex systems representations that include elements of theory-based evaluation approaches. The Commission also favors specifying evaluation questions that are "used as starting point in the preparation of terms of reference." The Commission is not generally prescriptive about methods and techniques, although particular "islands" within the Commission have their own favorites. For example, particular economic models are favored in one Directorate General, while a different economic model will be favored elsewhere. Because of the strength of the accountability rationale for evaluation, there is a tendency to formally favor indicators and quantification where possible.

The Institutional Setting. The Commission's evaluation system is decentralized: "every operational DG should have a designated evaluation function; and every operational DG should establish an annual evaluation plan identifying programs which will be the subject of an evaluation" (EC SEC 1051, 2000). These separate units have been networked together and coordinated by DG BUDGET (and since 2009 by the Secretariat General). In 2007 it was estimated that in total there were 140 staff (full-time equivalents) dedicated to evaluation across all directorates general of the Commission.

Evaluations are almost always outsourced following standard procurement procedures. There has been a trend in recent years toward framework contracts awarded to consortia of contractors for up to three years, albeit with built-in competition. That is, more than one potential contractor is selected for each block of work.

Most evaluations of any scale also have a steering group with members drawn from operational departments, the evaluation function itself, an evaluation expert from elsewhere in the Commission, independent experts, and stakeholders likely to be affected by an evaluation. Steering groups are expected to keep an evaluation to its terms of reference, facilitate access, clarify interpretations and conclusions, and facilitate dissemination and follow-up.

Until recently, independence has not featured as a strong theme in policy-level discussions of evaluation. It has mainly been deployed as an argument against contractors with potential conflicts of interest. Recently, with elaboration of the Commission's own evaluation standards (Annex II to EC SEC 213, 2007), independence has at least been mentioned. Standard C 12 states that "the evaluator's independence in his/her work must be respected and the evaluation results must not be interfered with." However, there is a widespread perception in the evaluation community that independence is not always highly valued.

The Main Purpose of Evaluations. As outlined in the Commission's own guidance to staff (Evaluating EU activities, 2004), the purposes of evaluation are:

* To contribute to the design of interventions, including input when setting political priorities.
* To assist in efficient allocation of resources.
* To improve the quality of the intervention.
* To report on the achievements of the intervention (i.e., accountability).

Until 2000 the primary purpose of evaluation was to improve management and delivery of programs rather than decision making: "The Communication on Evaluation from July 2000 indicated that a better integration of evaluation into decision-making is one of the means to consolidate and improve evaluation practice within the Commission" (Evaluating EU activities, 2004). Most recently this has extended to the expectation that evaluation should be useful for "setting political priorities."

Evaluation Follow-Up. One of the main responsibilities of the decentralized evaluation functions and steering committees is to ensure follow-up and dissemination of evaluation results. There is growing emphasis on "use of evaluation"; studies on use have been commissioned, and utilization was the theme of the 2007 Communication.

The most formal follow-up process is a *fiche contradictoire*, commonly used in many national administrations, which operational managers have to fill in to explain their response to evaluation recommendations. In addition, dissemination is pursued through publishing reports on Commission Websites (Article 255 of the Amsterdam Treaty assumes public access to all documents unless there are exceptional reasons to withhold), public and sectoral seminars, presentation to internal cross-Commission networks, and using results in budget proposals and planning future initiatives, as required by the financial regulations.

Evaluation and EU Reform

The ongoing expansion, diversification, and institutionalization of evaluation in the EU, which began in the 1980s, have been given added impetus since the late 1990s through reforms of EU institutions. Evaluation has become a key element in day-to-day operationalization of reform.

Following the problematic Santer Presidency, Romano Prodi came to office as Commission President in 1999, committed to institutional reform to improve decision making, management, and policy making. Initiatives begun under Santer were taken on board and reinvigorated. "Promoting new forms of European governance" was one of the four strategic priorities of the Prodi Commission. The process of EU governance reform and modernization initiated in the early years of Prodi's Presidency is still ongoing today.

The *White Paper on European Governance* (EC COM 428, 2001) was given added urgency following Ireland's rejection of the Nice Treaty. The Commission's analysis of this crisis linked failures in EU governance, and in particular lack of transparency and openness, with the rejection by Europe's citizens of future political initiative.

The White Paper is addressed to all EU institutions and partners and seeks to articulate a common agenda: "The Commission cannot make these changes on its own, nor should this White Paper be seen as a magic cure for everything. Introducing change requires effort from all the other Institutions, central government, regions, cities, and civil society in the current and future Member States" (executive summary). The White Paper identifies five principles that underpin good governance: openness, participation, accountability, effectiveness, and coherence. Evaluation has found a place within the operationalization of most of these principles in the follow-up to the White Paper.

Governance, as it is understood in the Commission, includes not only decision making and public management but also new relationships between citizens and policy makers. The latter was seen as necessary because of citizens' evident lack of confidence in the political elite and the consequent reduced legitimacy of European institutions. This is captured in the Strategic Objectives 2005–2009: "All European institutions must adopt the mindset of being at the service of the citizens: Inherent in the idea of partnership is consultation and participation" (EC COM 12, 2005).

The most important reform-type developments that occurred in the early years of the 21st century included introduction of:

- Impact Assessment, seen as a key tool for improving policy making in the Commission, Parliament, and the Council, reinforcing coordination and making it easier to communicate decisions (EC COM 12, 2005).
- Activity-based management (and, in parallel, activity-based budgeting), a form of results-based management in the Commission that, together

with strategic planning and programming, links all activities with policy objectives and resource allocation.

• Alternatives to legislation, promoted in the action plan that followed the *White Paper on Governance,* suggesting that as well as streamlining legislation, sometimes nonregulatory instruments might be appropriate (see also EC Report from the Commission, 2007).

Impact Assessment (IA) is especially significant. The IA procedure appraises options in major policy proposals, from an economic, social, and environmental perspective. It is intended to contribute to effectiveness and transparency and to "improve the quality and coherence of the policy development process." Following the Göteborg Council of 2001, sustainable development—economic, social, and environmental—became the overarching priority across all EU policies. As the evaluation of the IA system noted, "the benefits of Impact Assessments are not limited to cutting red tape for business"; rather, it is "intended to seek to assess alternative policy options and their likely positive and negative impacts in all relevant spheres" (Evaluation Partnership, 2007).

Given the way evaluation has been tied into the reform process, evaluation in the EU has faced two kinds of challenges. First, it has become more integrated into decision making and policy making, strengthening concerns about its independence. Second, the reform process has itself reshaped the objects that evaluation has to analyze, mainly in terms of a new set of policy instruments, less amenable to conventional evaluation toolkits.

New Policy Instruments

The period of EU reform since the late 1990s has seen the emergence of a number of "new" policy instruments alongside legislation that goes beyond Vedung's typology (1998) of "carrots," "sticks," and "sermons."

The Character of New Policy Instruments. New policy instruments partly follow from resistance to overly complex regulation and from the view that deregulation supports competitiveness. These instruments were shaped by the dynamics between the EU's main institutions (the Commission, Parliament, and Council), with one institution taking the lead in some cases but not in others, and with all outcomes resulting from negotiation and compromise.

The new generation of policy instruments includes:

• Co-regulation initiatives that specify broad intentions but leave detailed regulation to national authorities.
• Self-regulation, for example, by trade associations and through voluntary agreements.
• More developed forms of consultation and dialogue intended "to improve the participation of interested parties" and to make "consultation more transparent."

- New forms of partnership and networking among the institutions of the EU, member states, and other policy actors
- More transparent use of expert advice in order to boost public confidence
- An open method of coordination, or OMC, which seeks to encourage pursuit of agreed policy goals through soft law (e.g., target setting, exchange of good practice, use of peer review), rather than formal legislation (see Zeitlin & Pochet with Magnusson, 2005)

Explaining the Emergence of New Policy Instruments. The drivers that underpin Commission reform and the emergence of new policy instruments can in part be understood in terms of contemporary ideas about good public management. Another possible explanation stems from the EU's substantive policy goals. This hypothesis would suggest that the kinds of policy goals the EU is pursuing require new kinds of policy instruments, which themselves require changes (reforms) in how policy making, implementation, and ultimately evaluation take place.

This hypothesis finds support in the content of the EU's strategic objectives (EC COM 12, 2005) and indeed the Lisbon Agenda, with its goals of growth, competitiveness, and sustainable development as agreed by the European Council of Ministers. These strategic objectives, under the broad headings of "Prosperity," "Solidarity," "Security and Freedom," and "Europe as a World Partner," would be difficult to address through traditional kinds of regulation and policy instruments, and certainly not without the active engagement of member states. In addition, these objectives are necessarily decentralizing because they require implementation tailored to diverse circumstances, they confront chronic problems that demand long-term action, and they imply cultural change as much as administrative fiat.

This depiction of EU policy and its connection to new policy instruments appears to resonate with generally accepted ideas about policy making described by Lindblom (1979) and Sabatier (1986), and about implementation (Hjern & Porter, 1981). These authors emphasize the negotiated and political nature of the policy making and regard implementation as part of the policy process.

Emergence of a more differentiated repertoire of policy instruments has undoubtedly extended the range of evaluation objects in the EU. This confronts evaluators with new methodological challenges: how to assess the contribution of these instruments to outcomes, often in settings where several policy instruments are simultaneously deployed in joined-up ways.

Implications for Evaluation Policy. Reforms and the emergence of new policy instruments located in the wider setting of EU inter-institutional dynamics has had direct implications not only for methodologies but also for evaluation policy, which since 2000 has seen:

- *A broadening of the scope of what is to be evaluated,* that is, a shift from evaluating only expenditure programs to all EU activities including legislation and variants of soft law, such as the OMC—an important part of the evolution of European policy making since the Treaty of Maastricht (Zeitlin et al., 2005; Tavistock Institute, Net Effect & IRS, 2005).
- *A shift in the focus of evaluation from the operational to the strategic* so that it can contribute to better policy making and coordination. As the Commission's evaluation guide for its own personnel puts it, "A better integration of evaluation into decision-making is one of the means to consolidate and improve evaluation."
- *An expectation that evaluation can demonstrate what has been learned about effectiveness of overall policies.* A recent innovation has been preparation of annual evaluation reviews (EC COM 300, 2008), which bring together results of evaluations into a summative judgment of the effectiveness of major European policies (EUREVAL & Ramboll Consulting, 2008). This is not without its downside; a shift toward the strategic priorities can reduce the perceived usefulness of evaluation to operational managers.
- *A new preoccupation with the evaluation of policies and aggregated activities.* There has been a discernable migration in the Commission over the last 15 years from a focus on evaluating projects to evaluation of programs and over the last 5 years at least to evaluation of policies. The Commission's staff guide to evaluation (Evaluating EU activities, 2004) contains a specific Annex on the Evaluation of Policies. However, tensions have emerged between what policy makers think they need and what evaluation theory and methods can deliver. As the 2007 policy Communication notes, "Due to the complexity of [such] ABB-activities, which often embrace several different policy instruments, it will most often be necessary to carry out individual evaluations at a more disaggregated level."
- *Wider distribution of evaluation responsibilities.* There has been a continuing push for other actors to take responsibility for evaluations previously undertaken by the Commission. At a micro level, the Commission has long adopted the practice of requiring projects and programs to undertake their own self-evaluations. Member state responsibilities to evaluate EU policies have also tended to expand. The Commission draws on the evaluations of others for synthesis reviews while also undertaking some policy-critical evaluations.
- *Joint working with member states.* In terms of governance reforms, European institutions see themselves as operating in partnership with member states. This applies also to evaluation arrangements and is expressed in a number of consultative and collaborative institutions. For example, a sectoral directorate general may set up "evaluation networks," bringing together those responsible for evaluation in that sector in member states, and also consult member states about EU evaluation terms of reference.
- *The spread of evaluation logics into other ways of managing within European institutions.* Evaluation thinking is now integral to many coordination and

management procedures. The OMC is essentially a form of self-evaluation by member states, drawing on a range of evaluative practices that include setting objectives and standards and peer-reviews. Impact Assessment (EC Impact, 2005), which bears some resemblance to an evaluability assessment, draws heavily on evaluation models such as intervention logics, logic models, etc. The European Court of Auditors, like many national audit bodies, now undertakes more audits that resemble evaluations and also uses evaluations in its audits (European Court of Auditors, 2005). Evaluation reports are central to many types of policy and management reporting.

- *Focusing on the uses of evaluation.* As in many institutions that evaluate, European institutions are concerned with the extent to which its considerable investment in evaluation is used and useful. Two major studies have been conducted by DG BUDGET of the uses of evaluation in the Commission. A recent study (EPEC, 2005) concluded that "the main users appear to be the officials directly involved with the implementation of the interventions that are evaluated. . . . Evaluation is less significantly used as an input to the setting of political priorities" (p. ii). The most recent communication on evaluation (EC SEC 213, 2007) focuses on evaluation use, especially as an input into policy making.

Some tentative hypotheses have been advanced about how reform in the Commission has affected evaluation and evaluation policy. However, one of the defining characteristics of the European project is its ambiguity. Identifying causal mechanisms is never easy; diverse explanations seem equally plausible, and indeed contradictory truths coexist. This mirrors the conflicting and coexisting narratives that underpin the European project.

Alternative Narratives for Building Europe

Debates about the project to build a political and economic Europe draw on different and conflicting narratives. These narratives encapsulate alternative understandings of what the EU is and how it might evolve. Narratives are partly a matter of practical politics—interest groups and political parties disagree and tell their own stories—but they have also been the subject of extensive theoretical and empirical study.[5] Two of the dominant EU narratives are supranational and two are more decentralized. Presentation of these narratives here is inevitably simplified.

Supranational Narratives: Federalist and Integrationist. The first supranational narrative is *federalist,* with a vision of future government based in Brussels and a division of powers between the federal authority and States. This narrative and vision for the future is not strongly advocated nowadays, even though it does persist, if only as a straw man that arouses angry reactions. The second supranational narrative, closer to the vision of Jean Monnet and Robert Schuman, sees the building of Europe as a slow but inevitable *integrationist* process that begins with economic cooperation (as with the European Coal and Steel Community) and eventually leads to political integration and unity. This narrative is underpinned by theories of functionalist and neofunctionalist spillover effects (Mitrany, 1965; Haas, 1958).

Decentralized Narratives: Intergovernmental and Multilevel Governance. The first of these is *intergovernmental*—alive and well in the EU from de Gaulle to Thatcher. It continues to assert national sovereignty and sees future relationships in Europe as structured forms of negotiation between states. The second more decentralized narrative is multilevel governance (Marks, 1993), a framework that recognizes the complexity of the EU as a polity in which states continue to be important actors but negotiate within new constitutional rules and alongside many other actors at subnational and supranational levels. This narrative treats the EU as an extant political system (rather than an entity in formation) and focuses attention on governance and on the EU's regulatory functions (Majone, 1996; Rosamond, 2000).

Co-Existing Narratives: An Uneasy Balance. All of these narratives coexist and come to the fore at different times, which goes some way to explain the ambiguities of the European project. This ambiguity is also reflected in the uneasy balance of power among the Council, the Commission, and the European Parliament. There is similar ambiguity in many other strands of European policy thinking: in the simultaneous commitment to respect diversity and national differences while encouraging convergence, and in a continued movement to create new supranational institutions while still advocating subsidiarity (devolving decisions to the lowest possible tier of government).

The language of the *White Paper on Governance* is often much closer to conceptions of multilevel governance than the more domesticated variants of governance thinking that characterize national discussions of public sector reform. Pollitt and Bouckaert (2004) observe that the Commission has not traditionally been receptive to contemporary public management thinking even though "they have shared some of the rhetoric ('decentralization,' 'performance')" (p. 233). However, the administrative actions that followed the White Paper are couched more in the language of conventional national public sector management. Unsurprisingly, differing narratives coexist within the Commission as in other EU institutions and parts of the Union.

Implications for Evaluation. These ambiguous and contested narratives have implications for evaluation policy, practice, and positioning in EU institutions. In particular:

- *Evaluation is itself a contested practice.* Some aspects of the Commission's evaluation portfolio can be understood as supporting an integrationist narrative, while other parts are more consistent with multilevel governance. An example of this might be advocacy of the OMC in some parts of the

Commission, with an explicit building in of evaluative methods around target setting and peer review among member states. A similar decentralizing intent can be detected in some Structural Fund evaluations.

- *Evaluation in EU institutions has been co-opted by the administrative branch.* The dominant role of the Commission makes it more likely that EU evaluations will be consistent with centralizing narratives, if only because the Commission is structurally more likely to be inward-looking than other institutions. If Parliament assumed a greater role, EU evaluations might become more firmly associated with decentralizing narratives.

- *Evaluation as a chip in the negotiating game.* Ambiguity is the lifeblood of negotiation. The complex functioning of the EU alongside competing narratives (or what one member state representative described as "EU smoke and mirrors—nothing is as it seems") underpins ongoing interinstitutional politics. It is possible to see association of evaluation with the rhetoric of public management reform, good governance, and "better regulation" as part of the interinstitutional political game. When the Commission emphasizes its commitment to a form of evaluation strongly associated with accountability, transparency, effectiveness, and efficiency, it is being consistent with the decentralizing narratives of multilevel governance but also showing commitment to an intergovernmental narrative ("How are *we* spending *your* money?"). Such a deployment of the evaluation chip as part of the ongoing political game could be seen as increasing the legitimacy of Commission activities, thus opening up space for other policy initiatives.

So, What Happens in Member States?

Assessing the differential impact of EU membership on evaluation across European states is beyond the scope of this chapter. What follows is a sampling of the kinds of effects that EU inputs and obligations have at the member-state level, based on available sources (Bedea, 2008; EVALSED, 2007; Ministry of Finance, 2009; Stern, 2006). This section should be read as mainly referring to those aspects of country-based evaluation directly linked with EU funding and competencies. Much else happens in evaluation that is not directly connected with the EU.

Evaluation Capacity Development Is a Relatively Recent Concern. There is some evidence that the impact of EU accession on evaluation capacity and practice has become stronger with each successive wave of new members. The compulsory obligation to evaluate in EU Structural Funds took effect only in 1988, and it was further strengthened in 1999. An explicit commitment in the EU to develop evaluation capacity dates from the mid-1990s. The first generation of evaluation guides, the *MEANS Collection,* was published in 1999. By the latest rounds of accession, in 2004 and 2007, evaluation capacity development was well planned and resourced. This probably had consequences for the speed with which evaluation became a priority for the new member states from Eastern Europe after 2004.

Country Circumstances Mediate EU Influence. Internal conditions in countries can affect and mediate the potential influence of the EU on evaluation uptake. Because Structural Funds are inversely related to per capita national income, the impact of EU accession and evaluation promotion was less for the wealthier countries of Europe. Denmark, the Netherlands, the UK, and Sweden appear to have been less directly influenced by EU accession than Ireland, Italy, and Spain (see EVALSED, 2007, for detailed discussion of Ireland, Italy, and the Netherlands). It was only with the onset of the public sector reform movement in the 1990s that evaluation took off in such countries as Denmark and the Netherlands (Furubo et al., 2002; Kickert & van Vught, 1995). Even among recent new members, such as Romania and Poland, early expansion of evaluation was limited until minimum civil service reforms were instituted as part of the transition from communism.

The federal structure of Spain appears to have acted as a barrier to generalized evaluation uptake, although this was probably also constrained by the slow reform of national administrations after the fall of the Franco dictatorship. Spain, however, has had pockets of good evaluation practice in particular sectors at the national level (outside of EU-funded programs) and also at the regional level. Spain is now showing signs of adopting evaluation more systematically at the central government level, having recently set up a national Agency for the Evaluation of Public Policy and Service Quality under the aegis of the Ministry of Public Administration (Vinas, 2009).

Germany, a founding member of what was then the Economic Coal and Steel Community, adopted a limited range of evaluation practices in the 1960s that only expanded with a substantial input of EU funds following German reunification. One condition that appears to be generally influential is the extent to which a country had occasion to deploy evaluation in management of an economic downturn when wishing to reduce public expenditure. Long periods of relative stability and prosperity probably slowed down institutionalization of evaluation in the Netherlands and Denmark as well as in Germany.

Another country-level contingency in Germany is the extent to which it has had a corporatist or consensus-driven political culture. A strong national consensus can offer an alternative mechanism for resource prioritization—one of evaluation's functions for governments. This probably also applies to the Netherlands, where the so-called polder model in its modern expression, following the Wassenaar Accords of 1982, aimed for consensus among government, employers, and trades unions. This accord is credited with underpinning the Netherlands' economic success of the late 1990s. (A similar argument has been advanced in relation to the consequences of direct democracy—and prosperity—in Switzerland, even though it is not a member of the EU.)

A strong commitment to evaluation in a national government can also multiply the EU effect. Thus, the Italian Treasury made a major (and successful) effort from the mid-1990s to improve evaluation capacity within Structural Funds across the country's regions. This involved setting up a dedicated unit that worked closely with and networked regional authorities and evaluators working within regions.

EU inputs, despite their undoubted importance, are not a transmission belt for evaluation. EU actions occur in diverse national contexts, some of which will be more conducive to evaluation uptake than others. As evaluators know, context matters!

Limited Expansion Outside Areas of EU Competence. EU-initiated evaluation can remain in a silo, not impinging on other nationally funded policies. This was the case in many countries that joined the EU (or its precursor, the European Economic Community) in the 1970s and 1980s (Ireland, Spain, Portugal, Greece). Ireland began to institutionalize evaluation competencies acquired in EU programs only in the late 1990s. However, this risk has been anticipated and addressed in the latest round of accession countries from Eastern Europe. Poland, Romania, and the Czech Republic are setting up an evaluation infrastructure that includes all ministries and policy areas from the outset. In Romania, for example, the National Evaluation Strategy 2007–2013 includes a review of national evaluation capacity and of legislation governing ministerial reporting and control, and a commitment that "evaluation be integrated into the procedures for the planning, delivery and follow-up of all public policies and programs by 2013, regardless of funding lines" (Ministry of Public Finance, 2006).

Where evaluation is introduced through EU Structural Funds, there appears to be a tendency for it to be centralized, usually being managed in the central government by the national treasury or ministry of finance. Evaluation can then become a vehicle for expenditure control. Arguably this is one reasonable purpose of evaluation. However, if national treasuries are the main locus for evaluation management and coordination, it does make for an evaluation nonculture. Certainly the diverse, socially engaged, decentralized, and often bottom-up evaluation culture in the UK, Sweden, and the Netherlands has not emerged so far among the newer members of the EU.

Effects on Evaluation Supply and Demand. Alongside an extension of evaluation activity, the EU's commitment to capacity building, along with countries' own efforts to meet their evaluation obligations, has had a more general impact on evaluation supply and demand. Among the major effects have been emergence of an evaluation market with a slow expansion of suppliers from among local firms, institutes, and universities; training and education delivered through awareness-raising events, short courses, and occasionally accredited university courses becoming a priority; and development of the evaluation community by supporting networks, seminars, and establishment of national evaluation societies, of which there are now more than 20 across the EU.

NEW DIRECTIONS FOR EVALUATION • DOI: 10.1002/ev

Conclusions

In this chapter, I have discussed how EU evaluation policies support the spread of evaluation across Europe. The big expansion of evaluative activity in EU institutions, overwhelmingly in the European Commission, has had multiplier effects for EU member states. In many member states that previously had no experience of evaluation, there is now an expanding and committed evaluation community.

The main impact of EU inputs has been at the central government level, and evaluation in the EU has become closely aligned with public management agendas. The reform and modernization movement in the EU institutions since 2000, at least rhetorically, has strengthened this alignment. Other changes, some associated with reform, such as better-regulation initiatives, have also led to proliferation of new policy instruments. These new instruments, often nonregulatory in character and deployed in partnership with member states, together with changes in substantive domain policies, have also shaped the way EU evaluation policy is evolving.

This chapter has underlined the extent to which the European project to build the Union remains political and often contested, explained by alternative and often competing narratives. It is against this background that EU evaluation policies should be understood. Evaluation in the EU and in particular in the European Commission has aligned itself to a public management and governance agenda that sets parameters for evaluation policy. Evaluation is seen as useful to decision makers and policy makers. As such, it is strong on utilization and perceived usefulness, and weak on independence.

The weak role of the European Parliament and the Council in EU evaluation further circumscribes the potential of evaluation policy. It would significantly change the present balance of priorities and purposes of evaluation policy in EU institutions if the Parliament had its own evaluation program.

There are also more general lessons about the diffusion of evaluation suggested by EU experience. For example, the circumstances of a number of countries affect evaluation uptake. Even when evaluation is a legal obligation, uptake will still be influenced by the national context. Institutional arrangements also influence evaluation uptake. The evidence suggests that evaluation is encouraged in supranational institutions, as in central governments, through certain kinds of reform. At the very least, some variants of evaluation are made possible by such reforms. Finally, the object of evaluation is also changing. There has been a shift in the EU to evaluating policies (rather than programs or projects) and also the emergence of new policy instruments. This requires new ways of organizing evaluations and new evaluation methods. I would argue that there is likely to be continuing contention about regulation (that is, how much of it we need). In these circumstances, new postregulatory, collaborative, coordinated, and consensus-building policy instruments will become more widespread, thus requiring continuing innovation in evaluation approaches, methods and policies, and not just in Europe.

Notes

1. A more detailed explanation of the role and functioning of EU institutions can be found on the Europa Web site (http://europa.eu/institutions/ inst/comm/index_en.htm).

2. This era coincided with experiments and innovations such as those associated with the U.S. War on Poverty and the UK's Community Development Programme (see Maris & Rein, 1967; Loney, 1983).

3. This policy seeks by investment and redistribution of resources to reduce disparities between the richer and poorer regions of the EU. Structural Funds more generally promote innovation and restructuring through developing human resources and infrastructure and promoting research and development.

4. See http://ec.europa.eu/regional_policy/sources/docgener/evaluation/ evalsed/index_en.htm.

5. This section draws on (but is not confined to) the helpful theoretical overviews of Ben Rosamond (2000) in his *Theories of European Integration.*

References

Bedea, C. (2008). *Evaluation standards and professionalisation in Romania.* Presentation at European Evaluation Society Conference, Lisbon.

Bienias, S. (2009, March). *Evaluation of structural instruments in Poland: Experience in evaluation capacity building.* Presentation at Evaluation of EU Structural Funds: Reinforcing Quality and Utilisation Conference, Vilnius, Lithuania.

Bosch, H. (2008, July). *Evaluation and parliamentary oversight.* Speech by chair of European Parliament's Committee on Budgetary Control to Evaluation Symposium, Strasbourg.

EPEC (European Policy Evaluation Consortium). (2005). *Study on the use of evaluation results in the Commission: Final report.* Brussels.

EUREVAL & Ramboll Consulting. (2008). *Meta-study on lessons from existing evaluations as an input to the review of EU spending.* DG Budget, European Commission, Brussels.

European Commission Section:

COM. (2001). *European governance: A white paper* (Document No. COM(2001) 428 Final). Brussels.

COM. (2002). *Communication from the Commission on Impact Assessment* (Document No. COM(2002) 276). Brussels.

COM. (2005). *Europe 2010—A partnership for European renewal: Strategic objectives 2005–2009. Prosperity, solidarity and security.* Communication from the president in agreement with Vice-President Wallstrom (Document No. COM(2005) 12 Final). Brussels.

COM. (2008). *Evaluation in the Commission reporting on results: Annual evaluation review 2007. Conclusions and findings from evaluations in the commission* (Document No. COM(2008) 300). Brussels.

Evaluating EU activities: A practical guide for the Commission Services. (2004). July DG BUDGET, Evaluation Unit. Brussels.

Financial regulation and implementing rules applicable to the general budget of the European Communities: Synoptic presentation and a selection of legal texts relevant to establishing and implementing the budgets. (2008). Luxembourg.

Impact Assessment Guidelines. (2005). Brussels.

Multi-annual overview of finalized evaluations classified per ABB-activity 2002–2007. (2008). DG Budget. Brussels.

Report from the commission on subsidiarity and proportionality (15th report on better lawmaking). (2007). Brussels.

SEC. (1996). *SEM 2000 communication on evaluation, concrete steps towards best practice across the commission* (Document No. SEC 96/659). Brussels.

SEC. (2000). *Strengthening evaluation of commission activities, communication to the commission from Mrs. Schreyer in agreement with Mr. Kinnock and the president according to action 16 of the action plan for reform focus on results* (Document No. SEC(2000) 1051). Brussels.

SEC. (2007). *Responding to strategic needs: Reinforcing the use of evaluation, communication to the commission from Ms. Grybauskaité in agreement with the president* (Document No. SEC (2007) 213). Brussels.

Statistical overview of commission evaluations. (2008). Brussels.

European Court of Auditors. (2005, November). *Audit guidelines on evaluation.* Retrieved July 13, 2009, from http://www.riksrevisjonen.no/NR/rdonlyres/874C9D2D-6A40–4580-BF92-E3AE939BFC47/0/ECAAUDITGUIDELINESONEVALUATION.pdf

EVALSED. (2007). Sourcebook on capacity development: Italy, Ireland and the Netherlands. In *Guide to evaluation of socio economic development.* DG REGIO. Brussels.

The Evaluation Partnership (TEP). (2007). *Evaluation of commission's Impact Assessment system.* Secretariat General of the European Commission. Brussels.

Furubo, J.-E., Rist, R. C., & Sandahl, R. (Eds.). (2002). *International atlas of evaluation.* New Brunswick, NJ: Transaction.

Haas, E. B. (1958). *The uniting of Europe: Political, social and economic forces 1950–1957.* Palo Alto, CA: Stanford University Press.

Hayward, J., & Menon, A. (Eds.). (2003). *Governing Europe.* New York: Oxford University Press.

Hjern, B., & Porter, D. O. (1981). Implementation structures: A new unit of administrative analysis. *Organization Studies, 2*(3), 211–227.

Kickert, W., & van Vught, F. (Eds.). (1995). *Public policy & administration sciences in the Netherlands.* Hemel Hempstead: Prentice Hall/Harvester Wheatsheaf.

Lindblom, C. E. (1979). Still muddling, not yet through. *Public Administration Review, 39,* 517–526.

Loney, M. (1983). *Community against government: The British Community Development Project 1968–1978.* London: Heinemann.

Majone, G. (1996). A European regulatory state? In J. Richardson (Ed.), *European Union, power and policy making.* London: Routledge.

Maris, P., & Rein, M. (1967). *Dilemmas of social reform: Poverty and community action in the United States.* New York: Atherton Press.

Marks, G. (1993). Structural policy and multilevel governance in the EC. In A.Cafruny & G. Rosenthal (Eds.), *The state of the European Community: The Maastricht debates and beyond* (Vol. 2, pp. 391–410). London: Longman.

Ministry of Finance, Republic of Lithuania. (2009, March). *Evaluation of EU Structural Funds: reinforcing quality and utilisation.* Conference proceedings. Vilnius, Lithuania.

Ministry of Public Finance, Romania. (2006, November). *National evaluation strategy.* Presentation at launch of national strategy. Bucharest.

Mitrany, D. (1965). The prospect of integration: Federal or functional? *Journal of Common Market Studies, 4,* 119–149.

Pollitt, C., & Bouckaert, G. (2004). *Public management reform: A comparative analysis.* New York: Oxford University Press.

Rosamond, B. (2000). *Theories of European integration.* Basingstoke, Hampshire: Palgrave.

Sabatier, P. A. (1986). Top-down and bottom-up approaches to implementation research: A critical analysis and suggested synthesis. *Journal of Public Policy, 6*, 21–48.

Stern, E. (2006, November). *Second Polish evaluation conference: Ex ante evaluation for structural policies, synthesis report.* Conference organized jointly by the Polish Ministry of Regional Development and the Polish Enterprise Agency. Warsaw.

Tavistock Institute, London, Net Effect Ltd., Helsinki, Istituto per la Ricerca Sociale, Milan. (2005). *Open Method of Co-ordination: How the Europe OMC worked—Implications for the co-ordination of policy under i2010.* Brussels: DG Information Society.

Vedung, E. (1998). Policy instruments: Typologies and theories. In M. L. Bemelmans-Videc, R. C. Rist, & E. Vedung (Eds.), *Carrots, sticks and sermons: Policy instruments and their evaluation,* New Brunswick, NJ: Transaction.

Vinas, V. (2009). The European Union's drive towards public policy evaluation: The case of Spain. *Evaluation: The International Journal of Theory, Research and Practice, 15*(3).

Wollman, H. (Ed.). (2003). *Evaluation in public sector reform: Concepts and practice in international perspective.* Cheltenham/Northampton: Elgar.

Zeitlin, J., & Pochet, P., with Magnusson, L. (Eds.). (2005). *The Open Method of Coordination in action: The European employment and social inclusion strategies.* Brussels: P.I.E.-Peter Lang.

ELLIOT STERN is professor of evaluation research at Lancaster University, United Kingdom, was previously a director of the Tavistock Institute in London, and edits Evaluation: The International Journal of Theory, Research and Practice. *He is a past president of the UK and European Evaluation Societies and has been a consultant and evaluation contractor to the European Commission since 1985.*

NEW DIRECTIONS FOR EVALUATION • DOI: 10.1002/ev

Leeuw, F. L. (2009). Evaluation policy in the Netherlands. In W.M.K. Trochim, M. M. Mark, & L. J. Cooksy (Eds.), *Evaluation policy and evaluation practice. New Directions for Evaluation, 123,* 87–102.

6

Evaluation Policy in the Netherlands

Frans L. Leeuw

Abstract

This chapter discusses the development of evaluation policy in the Netherlands. It distinguishes between several periods: the 1970s and before, when there was little or no evaluation, much less evaluation policy; the late 1970s and 1980s, when evaluation increased but there was still little formal policy; the 1990s, when the government began to establish its formal evaluation policy; and the current decade, when evaluation policy was further formalized and evaluation activities blossomed. The author shows that the Dutch policy has always been rather liberal, leaving much room to the community of professionals. The chapter concludes with a summary of the current state of evaluation policy in the Netherlands, showing that the critique on evaluations and the two other strands of activities that produce "evaluative feedback" (i.e., performance auditing and inspection/oversight) is increasing. © Wiley Periodicals, Inc.

This chapter analyzes the development of evaluation policy in the Netherlands. The Netherlands is a small country of 33,883 square kilometers and a population of 16.5 million. In 2007, the GDP was $687 billion (https://www.cia.gov/library/publications/the-world-factbook/geos/nl.html).

Note: I wish to thank Mel Mark and Bill Trochim for their comments on an earlier draft. In particular, I want to thank Leslie Cooksy for her suggestions regarding analysis of evaluation policy in the Dutch context and especially for her editorial recommendations.

NEW DIRECTIONS FOR EVALUATION, no. 123, Fall 2009 © Wiley Periodicals, Inc., and the American Evaluation Association. Published online in Wiley InterScience (www.interscience.wiley.com) • DOI: 10.1002/ev.307

It is a constitutional democracy and has a central government (comprising a dozen ministries with some 120,000 civil servants), many executive agencies that work at arm's length from the central government, several hundred municipalities, and a dozen provinces. Parliament consists of two chambers. Its government is no less complicated than any other national government, but the size of the Netherlands makes it a natural laboratory for studying the evolution of evaluation policy from little or no evaluation activity to the mature evaluation culture described in Furubo, Rist, and Sandahl (2002).

The chapter considers both formal and informal (unwritten) evaluation policies as well as tracks important changes that have taken place over the last decades. The discussion distinguishes several periods: (1) the 1970s and before, when there was little or no evaluation, much less evaluation policy; (2) the late 1970s and 1980s, when evaluation increased but there was still little formal policy; (3) the 1990s, when the government began to establish its formal evaluation policy; and (4) the current decade, in which evaluation policy has been further formalized and evaluation activities blossomed. The chapter ends by summarizing the current state of evaluation policy in the Netherlands and looking forward to the future.

There are two key Dutch governmental institutions relevant to understanding evaluation in the Netherlands. The first is the National Audit Office (*Algemene Rekenkamer,* hereafter referred to as NAO), which is responsible for conducting audits of government agencies and programs. It serves both the legislative and executive branches but is independent. In terms of its activities, it is equivalent to the U.S. Government Accountability Office (GAO). The second is the Ministry of Finance, which has as its mission to guard the treasury and aim for a financially sound and prosperous state of the Netherlands. Its Inspectorate of Public Finances reviews budget proposals from ministries in terms of their efficiency and effectiveness. The Budget and Accounts Act, originally passed in 1927, describes the responsibilities of both the NAO and the Ministry of Finance.

The Early Years: No Evaluation Policy and Little Attention to Evaluation

During his inaugural address at the University of Twente, Professor Andries Hoogerwerf (1977) presented baseline information on evaluations that had been carried out during the mid-seventies in the Netherlands. He reported that no more than 1 to 2 million euros were spent on evaluation annually, while the national budget was €40 billion. In contrast, approximately 2% (€1 billion) of the annual budget was spent on "research and development," including the universities, professional education institutes, and the national science foundation. Hoogerwerf accused the Dutch government of neglecting the importance of evaluation and of having neither a policy nor a vision for evaluation. His claim is supported by the absence of any mention of evaluation in the Budget and Accounts Act at that time (1927, revised 1976).

NEW DIRECTIONS FOR EVALUATION • DOI: 10.1002/ev

Although one of the act's articles indicated that performance and efficiency "investigations" *could* be carried out by the central government and the NAO, in practice only a few "performance audits" were done before 1970 (Dolmans, 1989).

What received much more attention from ministries, municipalities, and provinces was social policy research, an endeavor that can be seen to some extent as a predecessor to evaluation. This type of research originated in the 1920s and 1930s and was fostered over time by several influences, among them (1) concerns about overpopulation, (2) the commitment to a model of government in which governmental actions are subject to a range of public enquiry procedures and the consent of virtually all interest groups, and (3) a belief in American applied sociology as exemplified by sociologists such as Paul Lazarsfeld, Robert Merton, Peter Rossi, and others. Under the leadership of the central government's Ministry of Education and Sciences and the Ministry of Science Policy, several national research programs were installed during the early 1970s to stimulate this type of applied (or policy) research. The programs, implemented collaboratively, focused on demography, health, the environment, and the labor market. They supported needs assessments in the fields of housing, health, social welfare, and migration; mapping of attitudes of the Dutch population about social problems; and other studies intended to help design policies and programs. Although the topics were largely developed bottom up by the research community, the two ministries had informal rules to guide selection of studies. To the extent that applied policy research overlaps with evaluation, these informal rules represent the beginning of an informal evaluation policy. (During the first part of the 1980s, these programs were terminated; see Sociaal Economische Raad, 1983.)

Note that there were no links established between the work of the two ministries on the one hand and the Budget and Accounts Act and the NAO on the other; accountability and program-oriented research remained different worlds. In the world of accountability, the Finance Ministry began to attend to evaluation policy by establishing the Commission for the Development of Policy Analysis in 1972 (Bemelmans-Videc, 2002). Its task was to "encourage both inside and outside the government the introduction of policy analysis and evaluation through educational, publishing, and advisory activities in cooperation with academics and other professionals working in these fields" (p. 94). Experiences with the U.S. Planning, Programming, and Budgeting System (PPBS) motivated the Finance Ministry to install this committee, but the committee's goal to stimulate effectiveness studies came too early and was not heard (Post, 2008). (Later, however, a Policy Analysis Unit, renamed the Policy Research Unit, was created within the Ministry of Finance.)

Up to this point the Dutch government focused primarily on social policy research, and evaluation policies were informal at best. However, during the latter part of the 1970s ex post evaluations, as opposed to needs

NEW DIRECTIONS FOR EVALUATION • DOI: 10.1002/ev

assessments and other research intended to inform development of programs, became more important. The Netherlands was hit with an increasing budget deficit. At the same time, politicians discovered that, despite several years of rather fundamental changes in Dutch politics and policies (largely caused by the then social-democratic focus on and belief in the malleability of Dutch society), not much was known about the *impact and successes* of the policies. Specifically, several parliamentarian enquiries carried out in the early part of the 1980s about the costs and benefits of postwar Dutch industry policy and housing subsidies emphasized the lack of evaluative knowledge. These two forces, the budget deficit, and lack of information about program and policy impact, helped to change the climate in favor of evaluations. Parliament turned out to be an important trigger for systematic evaluations in the Netherlands. Reinforcing the Parliamentary focus, a high-level committee (named after its chairman, Vonhoff) established to advise on the structure of the Netherlands central government also referred to the limited attention paid to evaluation in its 1980 report.

The 1980s: The Birth of Systematic Evaluation and Evaluation Policy

In the 1980s, evaluation blossomed in the Netherlands, and informal evaluation policy not only was formulated but began to evolve into formal policy. As described below, this dramatic transition can be attributed to four factors: (1) demands by Parliament, (2) new vigor in the NAO, (3) the New Public Management movement, and (4) the Dutch administrative culture.

Parliament. The critique from Parliament about the lack of evaluative knowledge possessed by the ministries and agencies can be framed in terms of the doctrine of ministerial responsibility (Visser, 2008). According to this doctrine, ministers in the Netherlands are responsible for everything civil servants *do* or *forget to do but should do*. Parliament criticized ministers in two ways: first, for not knowing what the costs and effects of policies were; and second, for not having installed arrangements to do evaluations and audits that could have provided this information. In 1984, Parliament accepted a resolution from member Den Ouden-Dekkers, stressing the importance of evaluations in developing and implementing new policies. Ministers started to react to this critique and began to define evaluations and audits as a way to prevent or reduce the bashing from Parliament. By organizing arrangements for doing and using evaluations and audits, ministers could no longer be accused of neglecting these prerequisites for sound policy making and implementation. Some ministries started to organize evaluations in specialized units within or at arm's length from the government; others largely outsourced this work.

Even though these arrangements clearly indicate the beginnings of formal evaluation policy focused on effectiveness, there was no discussion in Parliament about the need for a formal governmental evaluation policy focused on accountability. It was believed that the Budget and Accounts Act sufficiently articulated the tasks and competencies of the NAO, the budget and control process, and the role of the Ministry of Finance. Further, it was believed that this act laid the groundwork for performance budgeting and auditing. It must be stressed that, in those years, what the NAO auditors and the Finance Ministry inspectors did was far from what was called evaluation, social policy research, or policy analysis. Again, there were hardly any links between accountability-focused and substantive policy-focused activities.

The National Audit Office (NAO). Although Parliament was not focused on accountability, another factor stimulating attention to evaluations was the awakening of the Netherlands NAO. This office had carried out financial audits since the early part of the 19th century, and although in principle the 1927 Budget and Account Act made it legally possible to do investigations dealing with efficiency and economy questions (Dolmans, 1989), before the 1970s it seldom used this gift (Leeuw, 1992). When in the 1980s a new president (F. G. Kordes) started an innovative line of performance audits that came to be known as *governmentwide audits*, this picture changed. These comparative studies were benchmarks, although the word was not yet used in the Netherlands' public sector. Every year the NAO carried out at least one such study. The studies inventoried and audited what government departments and agencies knew about the economy, efficiency, and effectiveness (the three Es) of their spending and their policy activities, with a focus on comparison and learning (Kordes, Leeuw, & van Dam, 1991). Publication of the first couple of governmentwide audits illustrated that the problems found in the two earlier parliamentarian enquiries into housing and the industry policy (see above) were *not* incidental. On the contrary, lack of evaluative information appeared to be endemic for many other domains of the central government.

The 1986 governmentwide audit found that information about financial costs and benefits of new laws was hardly available, despite the fact that hundreds of new laws were implemented over a couple of years and even though the Budget and Accounts Act urged ministries to have this kind of information available. Then, in 1988, it turned out that, of the more than 700 central government subsidies and grants, ministries had information on the three Es for only a tiny fraction of them (Leeuw, 1998). Further, in 1989 it was discovered that 28 inspectorates (active in measuring and stimulating compliance with rules and regulations in such fields as education, health, labor conditions, development aid, traffic, and waterworks) knew little about the impact of what they were doing and how it related to the costs involved. Some of these organizations did not even know which laws they, according to the NAO,[1] had to inspect (de Leeuw et al., 1990). In 1990, similar findings were produced regarding the oft-used policy instrument known as information and persuasion campaigns. Of the 70 campaigns that were implemented between 1985 and 1988 by the Dutch government, fewer than 10% were evaluated using methodologically sound approaches. The audit also found that there was only one campaign that was at least somewhat effective (van der Mei, Bukkems, Leeuw, & Rozendal, 1991).

The NAO governmentwide audits served as an incentive to get evaluations going in a systematic way. Because the NAO is a public institution, established by the executive and the legislative branches of the Dutch government, one could argue that the institution was framing the beginnings of an evaluation policy for the Netherlands. However, the policy would have to be considered informal because the Audit Office does not have legislative or policy-making tasks or responsibilities.

New Public Management Movement. A third explanatory factor was the marching in of New Public Management during the 1980s. This implied more attention to transparency, accountability, and the three Es, and it also helped change governmental structures by means of privatization, contracting out, and establishing executive agencies at arm's length from the central government (van Thiel, 2000). Implementing these changes created a desire to know what the benefits for the government budget were in terms of reduced transaction costs and other benefits. Finding little information on these costs and benefits stimulated ministries to press for evaluations of the effects of organizational changes. In particular, a new form of study, known as *reconsideration studies*, began to proliferate starting in 1981. The studies were largely desk research done by departmental study groups. A crucial element in these studies was that every report had to have a section describing a minus 20% budget option and its consequences for policy making and society. The central characteristic of the minus 20% option was that the report had to specify what the consequences would be of such a budget cut, for efficiency and—in particular—for goal achievement of the policy under review. A report could not be published and discussed by cabinet and Parliament unless such a section was part of it. This approach was linked to the more general idea of zero-based budgeting. Hundreds of these studies have been carried out since 1981. (Since 1994, these studies have been called "interdepartmental policy studies.")

Administrative Culture. A fourth factor behind the sudden growth in the number of evaluations is the administrative culture of the Dutch government (Bemelmans-Videc, 2002), which is generally believed to be exceptionally open to innovation. Although a fair proportion of the decision makers in the Dutch government are jurists, one can also find sociologists, administrative scientists, and economists. These more data-oriented decision makers created an atmosphere in which evaluation easily could "move in and move on" (Bemelmans-Videc, 2002, p. 95). This also helped to develop an administrative culture in which evaluation was seen as a way to learn from earlier mistakes instead of as a mechanism to reduce the heat from Parliament. The response of the Ministry of Education and Sciences to Parliament's 1984 resolution on program evaluation (mentioned above) demonstrates the change in how evaluation was viewed. In 1986, the ministry installed a Committee on Program Evaluation. Summarizing its final report in 1992, Bemelmans-Videc said that the committee "pleaded for the institutionalization of the evaluation function in government practice, emphasizing the important societal values that evaluation represented. The report also suggested the outline of how evaluation of policy and its implementation should become part of society's cultural attainments" (p. 95).

The 1990s: Formal Evaluation Policies Created

All these developments and the subsequent growth in the number of evaluations and money involved led the NAO in the early 1990s to focus one of its governmentwide audits on the evaluation infrastructure of the Dutch government. Specifically, it looked into the role, functions, costs, and utilization of 150 randomly selected empirical evaluation studies, and it inventoried which organizational structures the ministries had put in place to guarantee production of independent evaluations. Although the component focused on evaluation utilization was done more in line with the academic literature (Weiss, 1998; Leeuw & Rozendal, 1994), the study resembled earlier GAO work (1987). (As the former head of the NAO's Performance Audit and Evaluation department, I met with Eleanor Chelimsky and Ray Rist at GAO Headquarters in Washington, DC, and found the GAO work so intriguing that we decided to implement a similar review of evaluation in the Netherlands.) The inventory focused on how departmental and semi-independent outside evaluation units were structured, what they did and with what results, what the infrastructure for evaluations looked like, how much the studies cost, how transparent the finances were, how the transfer of information to politicians and senior civil servants took place, and finally how much evidence there was of instrumental and cognitive utilization of the selected evaluations (Mulder et al., 1991). For some ministries the results were negative, for others much more positive. Either way, the governmentwide audit called attention to the structure and processes of evaluation, not just its availability or quality.

Policies on the Definition of, Need for, and Location of Evaluation. The governmentwide audit triggered creation of the *Cabinet Memorandum on Policy Evaluation* of 1991. It is only nine pages long and says that:

- Policy evaluation, including developing and using performance indicators, is important and so is policy evaluation research.
- There is no need to develop a law about managing evaluation. (Evaluations were already mentioned in the Budget and Accounts Act and in several other administrative documents, and that was believed to be enough.)
- Systematic evaluation must be a continuous part of any policy process, but evaluations are believed to be particularly relevant when market signals are not available or not effective.

- Evaluation (as well as policy analysis) can help inform policy choices.
- Evaluations should be carried out as much as possible in the regular departmental and ministerial processes surrounding the budget process.
- Having evaluations done is a core responsibility of political and administrative top management.
- Performance indicators and performance monitoring is as much a form of policy evaluation as are specific studies or policy evaluation research.

The memorandum also held a plea for doing more evaluations of laws and legal procedures.

The Dutch cabinet outlined a number of strategies to realize these goals:

- Giving evaluation a more prominent role in the Budget and Accounts Act and redesigning some lower-level regulation
- Installing departmental evaluation groups tasked with programming and planning evaluations
- Producing an annual report in which the ministries had to make clear which evaluations are intended and in process, what the results have been, and how these have been used in budgetary decision making
- Making the central financial and economic affairs directorates of the ministries responsible for stimulating and coordinating the evaluation functions and checking the costs and benefits of evaluations.

Consistent with Trochim's definition of evaluation policy as "any rule or principle that a group or organization uses to guide its decisions and actions when doing evaluation" (this issue), the cabinet has clearly laid out a nontrivial set of principles about evaluation policy, despite the generality of the memorandum. Although specifics involving methods, standards, and types of utilization and learning are left to the ministries, agencies, and in particular the evaluation units themselves, the memorandum has pressured ministries and organizations to create formal evaluation units. Additional pressure was created by the knowledge that the NAO would do follow-up audits to learn how the evaluation infrastructure of the Dutch government developed over the years.

Although the memorandum has indeed been taken seriously, the substance has been only partly implemented. With some exceptions, central evaluation groups within the ministries were not created, the role of the financial and economic affairs directorates never became as important as the memorandum suggested, and information on costs and use of evaluation was made available only slowly. However, evaluations of laws indeed were carried out more often, largely because of the implementation of sunset legislation and sunset policies in the 1990s and 2000s (Klein Haarhuis & Niemeijer, 2008). Because there is an annual increase of some 75 laws (and a total of approximately 1,800 existing laws), sunset legislation created a rather strong push factor for policy makers to get involved in evaluations.

NEW DIRECTIONS FOR EVALUATION • DOI: 10.1002/ev

Monitoring instruments resembling national surveys in the United States are carried out regularly on such topics as health, social integration, education, and victimization, among others, and also increased in number. For example, in the field of social integration of ethnic minorities, some 20 monitoring instruments exist (Kulu-Glasgow, Leeuw, Uiters, & Bijl, 2007).

Liberal Policies About Technical Quality. Although the policy is clear about the need for evaluation, there is limited attention paid to the methodological quality of evaluations and the setting of standards. Methodological debates hardly took place and the government position was liberal, stressing that the community of evaluators and social scientists were believed to be best positioned to guarantee that work of high methodological quality was delivered. The Polder model that characterizes much of Dutch politics (van der Knaap, 2000; van Hoesel, Leeuw, & Mevissen, 2005) explains, at least partially, the absence of methodological quality standards from the cabinet memorandum. The central element of this model is that decisions on government actions are subject to a range of public enquiry procedures and the consent of virtually all important interest groups. Participants are taken seriously, their opinions are listened to, and they sometimes do their own appraisals of new or proposed policy. In addition to the process of public enquiry, the largest and most vigilant stakeholders (like large corporations or semipublic-sector agencies) are engaged in ex post evaluations they commission themselves. (An example is Amsterdam-Schiphol Airport, which is active as a stakeholder when evaluations of the impact of expansion of runways on noise production and the health and well-being of surrounding areas are carried out.) One effect of the Polder model of government in the Netherlands has been that social acceptance of instruments and standards is more important than methodological quality of evaluations.

Performance Measures as a Form of Evaluation. By the end of the 1990s, the cabinet also took the first steps to develop performance measures of key activities as indicators of the effectiveness of policies. The objective was to provide insight into the effects of policies within society, both ex ante and ex post. In 1998–99, ministries started to include performance targets in their budgets (van der Knaap, 2000). Also a new style of government budget was implemented. It was designed to give answers to three simple questions: What do we want to achieve? What will we do to achieve it? What will be the costs of our efforts? In each fiscal year, the government's annual report has to answer the equivalent to these questions: Have we achieved what we intended? Have we done what we should have done in achieving it? Did it cost what we had expected? (van der Knaap, 2000).

Other Policy Developments. Three other developments related to evaluation policy occurred in the 1990s. First, the number of inspectors-general (IGs) and other oversight organizations grew rapidly. Data comparing the number of organizations, budgets, and numbers of personnel between 1989 and 2006 report a growth factor of three (Willemsen, Leeuw, & Leeuw, 2008). Important drivers of this growth were privatization of parts of the public sector (e.g., railways, financial markets, health, higher education, etc.), which led to establishment of new watchdogs (regulators); and several accidents with serious social consequences, which created pressure on the IGs to become larger, more active, and more productive. In addition, professional evaluation societies, both inside the Netherlands and on the European level, were created. The Netherlands played an active role in establishing the European Evaluation Society (EES) in the early nineties. The first (interim, pending an election) president of EES was the then president emeritus of the NAO Kordes, and the office housed the EES secretariat for a couple of years. The founding conference of EES was held in the Netherlands in 1994 (EES, n.d.). However, it took almost a decade before the Dutch Evaluation Society was established in 2001. These developments informed politicians and policy makers not only about the international relevance of this type of work but also about the structures for managing evaluations in other nations. Thirdly, increasing demands from the European Union to carry out evaluations also increased the amount of and attention paid to evaluation (Bemelmans-Videc, 2002; Leeuw, Toulemonde, & Brouwer, 1999; Summa & Toulemonde, 2002).

The 2000s: Increased Formalization of Policy and Increased Evaluation Activity

Dutch evaluation policy in the 2000s continued trends started in the 1990s. After the millennium change, evaluation and related activities such as inspection and oversight continued to thrive, with new actors appearing on stage. For example, the National Safety Board defines its analyses of accidents as a form of evaluation research because investigating accidents includes evaluation of compliance with rules, regulations, and other social arrangements (Mertens, 2008). Additionally, some 200 new municipal and provincial audit offices, though often very small, were established. Not only were there more evaluation-related entities and activities, evaluation policy also became more specific. In 2001, the Budget and Accounts Act was changed, making evaluation and related activities formally more important. This change was further articulated in a periodic circular (Regeling prestatiegegevens & evaluatieonderzoek Rijksoverheid, or RPE, 2001, 2004). In both documents the following topics were addressed in a more formal and articulated way than before. It was decided that ministries and agencies (1) have to be clear about balancing the use of different types of evaluative activities, (2) should be more explicit about the use of ex ante evaluations, (3) should be more explicit about the frequency with which evaluations are done, (4) should have an eye for methodological-technical aspects of evaluations (and look-alikes), (5) should help organize the transfer and utilization of evaluation findings to the top of the ministries and agencies, and (6) should make organization of and responsibilities for evaluation (and look-alikes) more transparent.

NEW DIRECTIONS FOR EVALUATION • DOI: 10.1002/ev

Another periodic circular on policy and program evaluation established the production of *beleidsdoorlichtingen,* or policy appraisals, somewhat comparable with the Program Assessment Rating Tool in the United States (Davies, Newcomer, & Soydan, 2006). Over the last 8 years, 23 of these appraisals have been carried out (Meyenfeldt, Schrijvershof, & Wilms, 2008). In 2008 a meta-analysis of the appraisals was conducted (Meyenfeldt et al., 2008), which found, among other things, that there are still large differences between ministries that take evaluation work seriously and those that see it largely as necessary duty. The meta-study also found that some ministries use independent evaluation institutes to do the groundwork for the appraisals (as requested in the circulars), while others define the work largely as internal-ministerial (i.e., bureaucratic) activities.

A relatively new development resembles Weiss, Murphy-Graham, Petrosino, & Gandhi's targeted or imposed use of evaluations (2008). Evaluation and accreditation committees have become more important, particularly in the fields of health, higher education, and crime and justice. These committees are engaged in doing or commissioning ex ante and midterm evaluations of higher education programs, behavioral interventions focused on preventing and reducing crime, health education programs, and interventions in other areas. These programs and interventions can be subsidized only if an ex ante evaluation has demonstrated plausibility with regard to the underlying theory and future impact. With regard to existing programs, continuation of government funding is dependent on the results of evaluations. It is this development that is also one of the engines behind the slowly but steadily increasing importance attached to *methodological criteria* when doing an impact evaluation of a program. The revised version of the Budget and Accounts Act and in lower-level regulation (RPE, 2004; CW, 2001) stimulated this attention. The approach outlined by the Campbell Collaboration is beginning to be discussed within several branches of the executive and legislative branches because of increasing awareness that process evaluations of interventions are rather different from impact evaluations. In the world of development aid programs, a similar movement is taking place, to some extent caused by the report "When Will We Ever Learn?" (Center for Global Development, 2006).

Finally, the pressure from the European Union to have nation states and their organizations get involved in evaluations has increased, sometimes as part of a compliance approach (are nation states doing what they are supposed to do?) and sometimes as part of a good governance approach (evaluation should be part of organizations). The expansion of the role and influence of the EU over the last decades refers not only to project evaluations, impact evaluations, and strategy evaluations but also to establishment of many monitoring centers and oversight organizations or inspectorates that work at the European level. This expansion has gone hand-in-hand with the booming business in evaluation. A side consequence has been development of several new professional evaluation societies in Eastern Europe.

NEW DIRECTIONS FOR EVALUATION • DOI: 10.1002/ev

The Current State of Evaluation Policy in the Netherlands

Davies et al. (2006) say that governments want evaluation to promote accountability and to improve governmental management. Looking to the Netherlands, one finds no doubt that the Dutch government has become more transparent and accountable and that evaluation and related activities have played a prominent role. Over the last two or three decades, an evaluation policy has been developed. (See Table 6.1 for an assessment of the state of evaluation policy in each of the categories outlined by Trochim.) However, there is weak policy enforcement and much space for what professionals think and do. It is also difficult to know the extent to which

Table 6.1. Extent of Evaluation Policy in the Netherlands, by Policy Type

Policy Type	Implementation in the Netherlands
Goals	Strong (at global level only): Goals, in the sense of statements of the importance of evaluation and expectations that will be carried out, have been set. However, they are at a fairly global level, open to interpretation, and some non-compliance is tolerated.
Participation	Moderate: Participation is largely open to those that want to participate. In this case, Dutch culture rather than evaluation policy assumes and requires an open process.
Capacity building	Strong: Financial resources have supported activities, at the ministry and agency levels. Specialized research centers working at the central government level and doing (and commissioning) evaluations have existed over the last couple of decades.
Management	Moderate: Circulars, cabinet memorandum, and some elements of the Budget and Accounts Act dictate aspects of evaluation management.
Roles	Little to none: Largely left open to the participants.
Process and methods	Little to none (other than those related to performance measures): But increasing attention is starting to be given to methodological criteria for impact assessments.
Use	Moderate: The governmentwide audits focused on evaluation use indicate at least an informal concern with use, but more recently "targeted use" (policies linking evaluation with accreditation and subsidization, for example) is in place.
Meta-evaluation	Strong: In earlier times governmentwide audits on evaluation infrastructure and use evaluated the evaluation policies associated with goals and management, but not process or methods. Over the last decade synthesis work is more and more on the agenda.

governmental management has improved as a result of the formal evaluation policy. Certainly management of *bureaucratic processes* has improved: more guidelines, protocols, rapid appraisals, monitoring, and other ex ante work are being done, and—if a little counterfactual history is permitted—that would probably not have been the case had the country continued to be in the pre-1970s mood. More uncertain is the effect of evaluation policy on the effectiveness of governmental policies and programs.

Some aspects of the Dutch experience explain the pattern of policy adoption described in the table. First, a governmental model that relies on extensive public input from multiple perspectives on decisions has, on the one hand, stimulated evaluation activity but has also made it difficult to discuss, let alone implement, evaluation policy related to methodological quality standards and criteria. The model also makes it more difficult (or less important) to put evaluation participation policies in place. Second, in the Netherlands, not unlike in the United States, evaluation activities and accompanying policy evolved on three separate tracks: (1) accountability-focused (the National Audit Office), (2) focused on inspections and oversight, and (3) focused on program development and evaluation. Gaps in evaluation policies might reflect the difficulty of developing a policy that applies across these three types of evaluative feedback. Third, the role played by the national evaluation society was small during the pioneering decades, but when it did develop it brought these three tracks together; it includes a membership of inspectors, auditors, and social science-trained evaluators. This suggests that the professional community sees the connections across the kinds of evaluative activities, even if the evaluation policy makers for a long time did not.

Looking Forward: Will Trends Continue?

"So far, so good" for the 2000s, would, at first sight, be the most obvious response to what has happened. Regarding development of a Netherlands evaluation policy, the trend seems to be toward an ever-more-formalized policy, and with regard to the evaluation activities themselves the trend seems to be toward a continued blossoming of variety and amount.

However, looking back from 2009, reality has been more complex. Indeed, Dutch evaluation policy is now more formalized than 15 years ago. Nevertheless, the language used by the regulators and lawmakers leaves much of the decision making to professional communities. Moreover, Dutch lawmakers often tolerate some noncompliance with rules and regulations, in particular when the consequences are believed to be not very important (for society or for them). My conclusion therefore is that the Dutch government is basically leaving evaluation policy to the professional community, although less so than a couple of decades ago.

With regard to evaluation activities, the assumption that blossoming would breed further blossoming has not been borne out. Over the last couple of years, the first signs of turning back from this trend can be detected. First, organizations (public and private, small and large) increasingly complain about the *performance paradox*: organizations that are best at conducting measurement, audits, and evaluations are not necessarily the most effective ones (van Thiel & Leeuw, 2002). Second, there are feelings of disappointment, because after all the investments in new public management, evaluation, auditing, and inspection (van der Knaap, 2000), there is still criticism of the efficiency and effectiveness of governmental actions because of accidents in hospitals, derailments, the lowering of educational performance of schools and pupils, and many more issues. The current financial crisis has only aggravated this feeling. This raises the question, Why haven't evaluation, auditing, and inspection helped us prevent these developments? Critiques of the sheer number and redundancy of public sector organizations doing this type of work have also reached Dutch shores, as has criticism of the administrative burden that inspections and auditing are causing (RMO, 2000; WRR, 2004). The frustration was further fueled by the IGs' acknowledgment that they did not know much about their own efficiency and effectiveness, although they did measure outputs (e.g., how many schools were inspected) and the level of satisfaction experienced by "inspectees."

The Netherlands central government in 2007 announced serious budget cuts for auditing (30% over a period of 4 years) and inspection and evaluation (20%), which were being implemented as of January 2009. Simultaneously, there is an opposing force that finds its roots in the EU and its continued demands for more evaluations, more audits, and more inspections. The consequences of these competing forces for evaluation policy in the Netherlands are not yet clear, but the trend toward more formal policy is likely to continue because of pressure on the national budget and an increased need for learning.

Note

1. The criteria this office uses are derived from laws and other regulations. Sometimes the office adds its own interpretations and perspectives.

References

Bemelmans-Videc, M. L. (2002). Evaluation in the Netherlands 1990–2000. Consolidation and Expansion. In J.-E. Furubo, R. C. Rist, & R. Sandahl (Eds.), *International Atlas of Evaluation* (pp. 115–128). New Brunswick, NJ: Transaction.
Center for Global Development. (2006, May). *When will we ever learn? Improving lives through impact evaluation* (Report of the Evaluation Gap Working Group). Retrieved August 18, 2009, from http://www.cgdev.org/files/7973_file_WillWeEverLearn.pdf
Commissie Programma Evaluatie. (1992). *Slotdocument: Uitnodiging tot evaluatieonderzoek [Final document: an invitation to evaluation research]*. Groningen: Author.
CW. (2001). *Comptabiliteitswet 2001* [Budget and Accounts Act 2001]. Den Haag: Author.

Davies, P., Newcomer, K., & Soydan, H. (2006). Government as structural context for evaluation. In I. Shaw, J. C. Greene, & M. M. Mark (Eds.), *The Sage handbook of evaluation*. London: Sage.

Dolmans, L.J.F. (1989). Naar supervisie en meer aandacht voor de doelmatigheid. De Algemene Rekenkamer tussen 1945 en 1988 [Supervision and accountability: The Netherlands Court of Audits from 1945 to 1988]. In P. J. Margry, E. C. van Heukelom, & A.J.R.M. Linders (Eds.), *Van camere vander rekeninghen tot algemene rekenkamer; gedenkboek bij het 175-jarig bestaan van de algemene rekenkamer* [Album of 175 years of the Netherlands Court of Audits] (pp. 377–431). Den Haag: SDU.

EES. *EES 10th anniversary*. (n.d.). Retrieved July 10, 2009, from www.europeanevaluation. org/download/?download=1&id=768733

Furubo, J.-E., Rist, R. C., & R. Sandahl. (Eds.). (2002). *International atlas of evaluation*. New Brunswick, NJ: Transaction.

Hoesel, P., van, Leeuw, F. L., & Mevissen, J. (Eds.). (2005). *Beleidsonderzoek in Nederland*. Assen: Van Gorcum.

Hoogerwerf, A. (1977). *Effecten van overheidsbeleid; Inaugurale Rede* [Effects of government policies: Inaugural address]. Enschede: Technische Universiteit Twente.

Klein Haarhuis, C. M., & Niemeijer, E. (2008). *Wet en werkelijkheid. Bevindingen uit evaluaties van wetten* [Law and reality: Results from evaluation of laws and regulations]. Den Haag: Boom Juridische Uitgeverij.

Kordes, F. G., Leeuw, F. L., & van Dam, J.H.A. (1991). The management of government subsidies. In A. Friedberg et al. (Eds.), *State audit and accountability* (pp. 280–299). Jerusalem: State of Israel Government Printer.

Kulu-Glasgow I., Leeuw, F. L., Uiters, E., & Bijl, R. V. (2007). *Integratiebeleid rijksoverheid onderzocht. Een synthese van resultaten uit evaluatie- en monitoringonderzoek 2003–2006* [Government's policy on social integration examined: A synthesis of results from evaluation and monitoring]. Den Haag: WODC. Cahier 2007–3.

Leeuw, F. L. (1992). Government-wide audits in the Netherlands. In J. Mayne et al. (Eds.), *Advancing public policy evaluation: Learning from international experiences* (pp. 131–139). New York: Elsevier Science.

Leeuw, F. L. (1998). The carrot: Subsidies as a tool of government—Theory and practice. In M.-L. Bemelmans-Videc (Eds.), *Carrots, sticks & sermons: Policy instruments and their evaluation* (pp. 75–103). New Brunswick, NJ: Transaction.

de Leeuw, G. van, Rietschoten, C., Strzelczyck, S.W.R., van Maurik, R., Venderbosch, R. F., & Leeuw, F. L. (1990). Inspecties en handhaving van wet- en regelgeving [Inspectorates and compliance with laws and regulations]. *Beleidswetenschap* [Policy Sciences], *4*, 238–254.

Leeuw, F. L., & Rozendal, P. J. (1994). Policy evaluation and the Netherlands government: Scope, utilization and organizational learning. In F. L. Leeuw, R. C. Rist, & R. C. Sonnichsen (Eds.), *Can governments learn? Comparative perspectives on evaluation and organizational learning* (pp. 67–86). New Brunswick, NJ: Transaction.

Leeuw, F. L., Toulemonde L. J., & Brouwer, A. (1999). Evaluation activities in Europe: A quick scan of the market in 1998. *Evaluation, 5*, 487–496.

Mertens, F. (2008). *Ongevallenonderzoek als vorm van evaluatieonderzoek* [Dutch Safety Board investigations as examples of evaluations]. Lezing, Vide Seminar. Den Haag.

Meyenfeldt, L., von, Schrijvershof, C., & Wilms, P. (2008). *Tussenevaluatie beleidsdoorlichting* [Mid-term evaluation of policy assessments]. Den Haag: Aarts de Jong Wilms Goudriaan Public Economics bv (Ape).

Mulder, H. P., Walraven, G., de Groot, A., Terpstra, F., Rozendal, P., Venderbosch, R., et al. (1991). Gebruik van beleidsevaluatie-onderzoek bij de rijksoverheid [Utilization of evaluations and the Dutch central government]. In *Beleidswetenschap* [Policy Sciences], *5*, 203–228.

Post, H. M. (2008). *Van IOO tot Rekenkamer. Als het goed is, zijn we niet geliefd.* Retrieved July 2, 2009, from http://www.basis-online.nl/index.cfm/1.123.448.0.html/Van-IOO-tot-Rekenkamer

Raad Maatschappelijke Ontwikkeling (RMO). (2000). *Aansprekend burgerschap. De relatie tussen de organisatie van het publieke domein en de verantwoordelijkheid van burgers* [Stimulating citizenship: The relationship between the organization of the public sector and the responsibility of citizens]. Den Haag, RMO.

Regeling prestatiegegevens en evaluatieonderzoek rijksoverheid (RPE). (2001, 2004). Den Haag.

Sociaal Economische Raad [Social and Economic Council of the Netherlands] (SER). (1983). *Nota en Reactie inzake de voorziening voor strategisch* arbeidsmarktonderzoek [Report and reaction regarding the organizational arrangement of strategic labour market research]. Den Haag, SER. Retrieved July 10, 2009, from http://www.ser.nl/~/media/DB_Adviezen/1980_1989/1983/b03417.ashx

Summa, H., & Toulemonde, J. (2002). Evaluation in the EU: Addressing complexity and ambiguity. In J. E. Furubo, R. C. Rist, & R. Sandahl (Eds.), *The International Atlas of Evaluation* (pp. 407–425). New Brunswick, NJ, and London: Transaction.

Thiel, S., van (2000). Quangocratization: Trends, causes and consequences. (Thesis.) Utrecht, ICS dissertations.

Thiel, S., van, & Leeuw, F. L. (2002). The performance paradox in the public sector. *Public Productivity and Management Review, 25*(3), 267–281.

Trochim, W. (2008, November). Evaluation policy and evaluation practice. (Presidential address.) Annual conference of the American Evaluation Association, Denver, CO.

U.S. Government Accountability Office. (1987). *Federal evaluation: Fewer units, reduced resources, different studies from 1980.* GAO/PEMD-87-9.

van der Knaap, P. (2000). Performance management and policy evaluation in The Netherlands: Towards an integrated approach. *Evaluation, 6,* 335–350.

van der Mei, W., Bukkems, G., Leeuw, F. L., & Rozendal, P. J. (1991). Instrumentele overheidsvoorlichting geëvalueerd: Resultaten uit een rijksbreed onderzoek [Evaluating persuasive government communication activities: Results from a government-wide audit]. *Openbare Uitgaven* [Public Finance], *24,* 192–201.

Visser, R. K. (2008). *In dienst van het algemeen belang. Ministeriële verantwoordelijkheid en parlementair vertrouwen* [At public service. Ministerial responsibility and parliamentary confidence. Den Haag: Boom Juridische Uitgeverij.

Weiss, C. H. (1998). *Evaluation: Methods for studying programs & policies.* Upper Saddle River, NJ: Prentice Hall.

Weiss, C. H., Murphy-Graham, E., Petrosino, A., & Gandhi, A. G. (2008). The fairy godmother—and her warts making the dream of evidence-based policy come true. *American Journal of Evaluation, 29,* 29–47.

Willemsen, F., Leeuw, F., & Leeuw, B. (2008). Toezicht en inspectie in maten en soorten [Oversight and inspection]. *Tijdschrift voor Criminologie* [Journal of criminology], *50,* 96–113.

WRR. (2004). *Bewijzen van goede dienstverlening* [Evidence of the quality of services]. Den Haag, SDU.

FRANS L. LEEUW, *director of the Research and Documentation Center, affiliated with the Netherlands Ministry of Justice, is currently the president of the Dutch Evaluation Society. He also is professor of law, public policy, and social science research at the University of Maastricht. Between 1987 and 1996 he was director of the Performance Audit and Program Evaluation Division of the Netherlands National Audit Office.*

NEW DIRECTIONS FOR EVALUATION • DOI: 10.1002/ev

Cooksy, L. J., Mark, M. M., & Trochim, W.M.K. (2009). Evaluation policy and evaluation practice: Where do we go from here? In W.M.K. Trochim, M. M. Mark, & L. J. Cooksy (Eds.), *Evaluation policy and evaluation practice. New Directions for Evaluation, 123,* 103–109.

7

Evaluation Policy and Evaluation Practice: Where Do We Go From Here?

Leslie J. Cooksy, Melvin M. Mark, William M. K. Trochim

Abstract

Three issues for evaluation policy and practice are described: evaluation policy dimensions, evaluation policy instruments, and the political and economic environment for evaluation policy. Selected future directions are outlined, including the need to describe the evaluation policy landscape, further articulate an evaluation policy taxonomy, and develop and implement tactics for influencing evaluation policy, with particular attention to the role of professional associations. © Wiley Periodicals, Inc.

If the context of evaluation practice is largely defined by evaluation policies, then evaluation policy gives us a way to think about systematically influencing that context. Through policy, such principles as technical quality, respect for people, and utility can be explicitly and systematically built into the evaluation expectations of an organization rather than being values we fight for, one evaluation at a time. Of course, it is never this simple (Julnes & Rog, 2007). To be a player in the world of evaluation policy making, we need to develop a language for communicating about types of

policies and strategies for influencing them. In this issue, Trochim lays out a theoretical framework and offers several ways of furthering our knowledge about evaluation policy. Calling for the American Evaluation Association (AEA) to continue its evaluation policy advocacy, Datta gives examples of professional organizations that have influenced evaluation (and other) policies and recommends strategies, such as coordinating with existing consortia of associations, to strengthen AEA's voice. Chelimsky discusses evaluation policies associated with the structure and location of the evaluation function in organizations and describes the kinds of policies needed to protect the independence of evaluators. Stern expands our thinking by examining the issue of evaluation policy from the perspectives and experiences of supranational organizations such as the European Union (EU). Leeuw's historical account of the evolution and increasing formality of evaluation policy in the Netherlands illustrates the role of culture in evaluation policy development.

These authors address various facets of evaluation policy and consider those facets in different settings, but plenty of territory to explore remains. To facilitate and prompt the next round of discussion, this final chapter describes some of the common and complementary themes about evaluation policy and outlines potential directions for next steps in understanding and influencing evaluation policy.

What Have We Learned?

This section focuses on three crosscutting issues: evaluation policy dimensions, evaluation policy instruments, and the political and economic environment for evaluation policy.

Evaluation Policy Dimensions. To guide study and development of evaluation policy, we need to know what dimensions or topics it encompasses. Trochim and Datta, in this issue, have started to define the limits and fill in the contours of the domain of evaluation policy. Trochim provides an eight-slice pie, while Datta draws on and adds to policy considerations found on the AEA Evaluation Policy Task Force (EPTF) Website (http://www.eval.org/EPTF.asp). When the two are compared, it appears that Datta's considerations begin to operationalize some of the slices in Trochim's pie. (Table 7.1 shows a rough correspondence between the dimensions in Trochim's framework and the issues identified by Datta.)

The absence of questions and issues that seem to line up directly with roles and use policies is not a comment on either the typology or the set of considerations. Instead, it is a two-pronged prompt for further exploration. We should ask whether these are the right categories, and at the same time we should think about how these categories can be further defined and articulated. Empirical research on what policies are already in place will be a critical step in refining our understanding of the domain of evaluation

Table 7.1. Match of Policy Types to Policy Questions and Issues

Evaluation Policy Types	Policy Questions and Issues
Evaluation goals	Evaluation definition (formal definitions and distinctions from functions such as program planning, monitoring, and performance measurement)
Evaluation participation (who is involved in *evaluation?*)	Who is involved (who is involved in *evaluation policy development?*)
Evaluation capacity building	Human resources (types of training, experience, and background required for evaluators)
	Resource distributions (distribution of capacity-building resources across diverse evaluation perspectives)
Evaluation management	Requirements of evaluation (when are evaluations required, what programs should have evaluations, how often are evaluations scheduled?)
	Evaluation budgets (standards for budgeting evaluation work)
Evaluation roles	
Evaluation process and methods	Evaluation methods (approaches recommended or required for what types of programs)
Evaluation use	
Evaluation of evaluation (meta-evaluation)	Evaluation ethics (policies for addressing ethical issues in evaluation)

policy. In the final section of this chapter, we identify specific ways to take these next steps.

Evaluation Policy Instruments. In his evaluation policy wheel, Trochim presents high-level policies as general statements that do not include operational specifications as the outer ring, with evaluation practice (the manifestation of policy) as the center. Moving from the outer ring to the center brings increasingly specific statements. At some point, the high-level policies are translated into policy instruments or strategies, which are in turn translated into practice. After reviewing several alternative classifications of policy instruments, Vedung (1998) proposes a set of three categories: "carrots" or economic incentives, "sticks" or regulatory constraints, and "sermons" or information.

In this volume, regulatory instruments are more frequently discussed than either economic or information strategies. For example, many of the details in the Government Performance and Results Act exemplify the stick, requiring annual collection and reporting of evaluative information on agency performance. Another example is evaluation set-asides, such as the set-aside for evaluation in the Public Health Service. Set-aside legislation could be considered an economic incentive because it provides resources for evaluation. However, as a regulation that requires agencies to use funds for evaluation that they might prefer to put toward programs, it is more of a stick than a carrot. Evaluation steering groups or evaluation units would be considered organizational strategies rather than policy instruments in Vedung's analysis (1998). But, for example, the European Commission requirement to have evaluation steering groups can be considered a regulatory policy instrument. Preferences given to evaluation proposals using certain kinds of designs and support for evaluation capacity-building activities are examples of economic policy instruments.

The information instrument, or sermons, is restricted to "no more than pure transfer of knowledge, persuasive reasoning, or exhortations . . . offered to influence the public or some segment of the public to do what government deems desirable" (Vedung & van der Doelen, 1998, p. 103). Leeuw illustrates the use of information as a policy instrument in the government's exhortations about the need to increase evaluation. Information could also be an instrument for Chelimsky's recommendations for policies about the kinds of knowledge that evaluators should have (of agency history and culture). The policies might be translated by encouraging evaluators to understand their surroundings and furnishing the information needed to do so.

Regulatory, economic, and information instruments begin to articulate how evaluation policies move from general statements to practice. It is perhaps not surprising that examples of implementing evaluation policy echo in kind the previous literature on instruments of (substantive) policy. To influence evaluation policy, evaluators will need a sophisticated understanding of policy instruments.

The Political and Economic Environment. Evaluation policy is made and implemented in specific political and economic contexts, whether organizational, national, or global. Organizationally, the political environment can be a threat to the independence and credibility of evaluation units; thus evaluation policy is needed for protection. At a global level, the EU's political environment (a coupling of supranational and decentralized politics in a system of multiple nations with their own histories, cultures, and interests) has created a demand for evaluation for the purposes of transparency and accountability, which has in turn generated several policies related to use of evaluation and its linkage to decision making. The development of sound evaluation policy may be especially important in a context of the economic uncertainties (uncertainties that some might say are the result of an absence of evaluation policy, especially policies about evaluation goals and use). Leeuw gives an example of the role of the economic environment in evaluation policy in the Netherlands:

"reconsideration studies," which were conducted primarily by internal ministry staff, were required to describe what would happen in terms of "goal achievement" if the budget for an intervention was cut by 20%. These examples indicate how evaluation policy reflects the political and economic environment and also has the potential to protect evaluation from political and economic threats.

Where Do We Go From Here?

Further conceptualization and description is needed to strengthen our ability to influence evaluation policy. This final section outlines next steps in conceptualization, description, and action.

Defining the Regions and Boundaries of Evaluation Policy. Through evaluation policy, evaluators are influenced by and can influence an entity's expectations for evaluation—its evaluation goals, its participants, its standards of quality, and so on. To understand the opportunities and limits of evaluation policy, we need to develop an understanding of the domain. An iterative process of conceptualization and description of the domain of evaluation policy could start with Trochim's eight categories (see Table 7.1). Then, empirical investigations could address questions such as:

- Do these categories apply equally across evaluation contexts and types?
- Are any categories missing?
- Are the categories at the same level of generality?

To answer these and other questions, description and documentation of existing policies are needed. An evaluation policy archive could inform conceptualization of the domain of evaluation policy and constitute a basis for exploring questions about policy implementation.

Identifying Effective Evaluation Policies. Ideally, a taxonomy and documentation of evaluation policies establishes a foundation for action, specifically by helping evaluators identify, create, and influence better evaluation policies (and to discuss, debate, and define what "better" means). Our first task, then, is to get a handle on what kinds and levels of evaluation policies are most appropriate under what circumstances. For example, both the Netherlands and the EU seem to have some clear policies about evaluation goals, but decisions about evaluation methods are either made as informal policies or delegated to the practitioners (Leeuw, Stern, this issue). Is this the result of a conscious decision to give priority to goals policies by formalizing them and not others, or simply an evolutionary process in which policies of equal priority are formalized sequentially? Evaluation theorists and those who do research on evaluation could lead the way in deepening our understanding of effective evaluation policy. In addition, evaluation journals could also encourage submissions on experiences with evaluation policies and the lessons drawn from those experiences.

As we collectively get a sense of the consequences of specific evaluation policies, our next task is to facilitate development of wise policies. Professional associations have a major role to play here. They can sponsor archives of evaluation policies, support professional development on evaluation policy at conferences and other events, and encourage networks for evaluators trying to influence policy. For example, AEA is about to release a Web-based platform that members interested in this kind of work could use to discuss and collaborate on evaluation policy research and development. In addition, professional associations can try to influence evaluation policy directly, as AEA has been doing for the last two years with its Evaluation Policy Task Force (EPTF). The EPTF is working with federal agencies on the executive branch side and with committee staffers and lobbyists in the legislative branch to try to influence federal policies on evaluation (see http://www.eval.org/EPTF.asp for more information).

As we raise consciousness about evaluation policy and encourage development of sound policies, we will also want to monitor the quality and implementation of the policies that are enacted. For this purpose, the kind of governmentwide audits that have been used in the Netherlands could furnish a model (Leeuw in this issue). A related task would be development of checklists and other measures to apply in these audits. Once the evaluation policy taxonomy has been further developed, it may amount to the basis for such measures.

Reprise

Evaluation policy shapes and defines our practice. As evaluators, we can influence the values expressed through evaluation policy, but only if we have a way to describe evaluation policies and policy instruments to policy makers, a sense of which evaluation policies are appropriate and effective, and facility with policy-influencing tactics. The ideas presented here and in the chapters of this issue of *New Directions for Evaluation* are only the first steps toward a more sophisticated understanding of evaluation policy and of strategies for developing and influencing it.

References

Julnes, G., & Rog, D. J. (Eds.). (2007). Informing federal policies on evaluation methodology: Building the evidence base for method choice in government sponsored evaluation. *New Directions for Evaluation*, no. 121. San Francisco: Jossey-Bass.

Vedung, E. (1998). Policy instruments: Typologies and theories. In M.-L. Bemelmans-Videc, R. C. Rist, & E. Vedung (Eds.), *Carrots, sticks, and sermons: Policy instruments and their evaluation* (pp. 21–58). New Brunswick, NJ: Transaction.

Vedung, E., & van der Doelen, F. C. J. (1998). The sermon: Information programs in the public policy process—Choice, effects, and evaluation. In M.-L. Bemelmans-Videc, R. C. Rist, & E. Vedung (Eds.), *Carrots, sticks, and sermons: Policy instruments and their evaluation* (pp. 103–128). New Brunswick, NJ: Transaction.

LESLIE J. COOKSY, *incoming president of the American Evaluation Association, is an associate professor at the University of Delaware where she directs a graduate program in evaluation.*

MELVIN M. MARK *is professor and head of psychology at Pennsylvania State University. He has served as president of the American Evaluation Association and as editor of the* American Journal of Evaluation *(now editor emeritus).*

WILLIAM M. K. TROCHIM *is professor of policy analysis and management at Cornell University and is the director of evaluation for the Weill Cornell Clinical and Translational Science Center, the director of evaluation for extension and outreach, and the director of the Cornell Office for Research on Evaluation.*

NEW DIRECTIONS FOR EVALUATION • DOI: 10.1002/ev

INDEX

A

Adams, B., 43

Adams, H., 43

AEA Evaluation Policy Task Force (EPTF), 18, 30, 36; AEA board and, 9; balancing tensions and, 9; evaluation policy areas identified by, 36–37; Evaluation Roadmap for More Effective Government and, 8; goal of, 8; health care reform and, 8; member feedback and, 9; national policy setting and, 8–9, 38–39, 108; Program Assessment Rating Tool and, 8, 18, 36; U.S. Office of Management and Budget and, 8, 38; website, 9, 104

AEA International and Cross-Cultural, Multicultural, and Indigenous Peoples Topical Interest Groups, 46

African Evaluation Association, 46

Aid to Families with Dependent Children (AFDC), 59–61

Alkin, M., 4

American Evaluation Association (AEA), 4, 8, 37, 45; globalization and, 46–47; meta-evaluation criteria and, 47; Obama administration and, 15, 30–31; Public Affairs Committees of, 9–10; Public Forums of, 9; role of, in national policy, 8–9, 35; 2008 annual conference of, 9. *See also* AEA Evaluation Policy Task Force (EPTF)

Aotearoa/New Zealand Evaluation Association, 46

B

Bedea, C., 79

Bemelmans-Videe, M. L., 89, 92, 93, 96

Bennett, C. J., 7

Bethell, T. N., 56

Bienias, S., 69

Bijl, R. V., 95

Bosch, H., 70

Bouckaert, G., 68, 78

Brouwer, A., 96

Brussels, evaluation in: evaluation focus and, 70–71; evaluation follow-up and, 72; evaluation purpose and, 72; forms of evaluation and, 71; institutional setting and, 71–72; legal and political basis and, 70

Bukkems, G., 92

Bureaucratic climate, 52–53

Bureaucrats, definition of, 53

C

Cahalan, M., 49

Carver, J., 25, 31

Carver, M., 25, 31

Center for Global Development, 97

Center for Public Program Evaluation, 8

Centers for Disease Control, 47

Challenges, for evaluation policy: ethical issues and, 28; illogical policies and, 27; overformalization and, 27; unintended negative side-effects and, 27–28. *See also* Evaluation policy

Chelimsky, E., 1, 8, 40, 49, 51, 57, 59, 66

Chen, H. 17

Christie, T. C., 5

Coalition for Evidence-Based Policy, 49

Congressional Record, 63

Consortium of Social Science Organizations (COSSA), 39

Cook, T. D., 5

Cooksy, L. J., 3, 12, 103, 109

Cousins, J. B., 18

Cross-branch politics, 52–53

CW, 97

D

Darling-Hammond, L., 49

Datta, L., 1, 6, 33, 50

Davies, P., 97, 98

de Leeuw, G., 91

Department for International Development, 5

Dimensions, of evaluation policy: evaluation budgets and, 36, 40, 42; evaluation definition and, 36, 40; evaluation ethics and, 36–37, 40–43; evaluation implementation and, 36, 40; evaluation methods and, 36, 40; evaluation requirements and, 36, 40; involvement in, 37, 41; issues corresponding to, 105 fig.; resource distributions and, 37, 40. *See also* Evaluation policy

Dolmans, L.J.F., 89, 91

Dominant professional culture, 52–54, 64

Donaldson, S., 5

Downs, A., 57

E

Early Head Start program, 5

Elkind, P., 4

Enron, 4

EPTF. *See* AEA Evaluation Policy Task Force (EPTF)

Eureval & Ramboll Consulting, 76

European Commission (EC), 68–74, 76, 78–79, 82

European Commission documents, 69–76

European Council, 74, 82

European Court of Auditors, 77

European Evaluation Society (EES), 46, 49, 96

European Parliament, 68, 70, 74, 82

European Policy Evaluation Consortium (EPEC), 77

European Union (EU): co-regulation initiatives and, 74; *Communication Responding to Strategic*

Needs and, 70; consultation and expert advice and, 74–75; as driver for European evaluation, 68; European Commission and, 68–74, 76, 78–79, 82; European Council and, 74, 82; European Court of Auditors and, 77; European Parliament and, 68, 70, 74, 82; narratives of, 77–78; Financial Regulations and, 70; Impact Assessment (IA) and, 74, 77; institutional reform and, 73–74; Lisbon Agenda and, 75; networking and, 75; new policy instruments and, 74–77; open method of coordination (OMC), 75–77; public sector reform and, 68; self-regulation and, 74; strategic objectives and, 75; Structural Funds and, 69, 79–81; transparency and, 74–75; *White Paper on Governance* and, 73–74, 78. *See also* European Union evaluation; European Union narratives, for building Europe; European Union evaluation, institutional reform and; European Union member states, evaluation and

European Union evaluation: Annex on Evaluation Policy and, 76; Brussels example, 70–73; as chip in negotiating game, 79; co-optation of, 79; as contested practice, 78–79; European Commission and, 68–74, 76, 78–79, 82; European Council and, 74, 82; European Parliament and, 68, 70, 74, 82; European Union narratives and, 77–78; European Union reform and, 73–74; lessons learned about, 82; *MEANS Collection* and, 79; scale and scope of, 69–70; Structural Funds and, 69, 79–81. *See also* Brussels, evaluation in; European Union evaluation, institutional reform and; European Union member states, evaluation and; Netherlands, evaluation policy in

European Union evaluation, institutional reform and: activity-based management and, 73–74; challenges and, 74; hypotheses about reform and, 75, 77; impact assessment and, 73–74; implications of, 75–77; instrument types and, 74–75; new policy instruments and, 74–77; nonregulatory instruments and, 74; sustainable development and, 74; *White Paper's* good governance principles and, 73, 78. *See also* European Union evaluation; European Union narrative, for building Europe

European Union member states, evaluation and: country vs. EU influence and, 80–81; Eastern Europe, 81; effects on supply and demand and, 81; evaluation capacity and, 79–80; Germany, 80; Italy, 81; limited expansion outside EU competence and, 81; Netherlands, 80–81, 97; Spain, 80; United Kingdom, 81. *See also* Brussels, evaluation in; European Union evaluation; Netherlands, evaluation policy in

European Union narratives, for building Europe: co-existing narratives, 78; decentralized narratives, 78; evaluation implications and, 78–79; supranational narratives, 77–78. *See also* European Union evaluation; European Union evaluation, institutional reform and

Evalsed, 79, 80

EVALTALK, 39

Evaluation Partnership, 74

Evaluation policy: all-encompassing aspect of, 14; analysis, 29; beliefs about program value and, 36; benefits for future evaluation practice and, 4; boat metaphor and, 34, 36, 47–48; challenges and, 27–28; characteristics of, 6, 15; as communication mechanism, 17; concern for, 14; consciousness and, 17; consequence and, 17; as creating organizational transparency, 17; culturally appropriate methods and, 45–46; debate over methods and, 4; defining boundaries of, 107; definition of, 4–5, 16–17; degree of implementation and, 41; as deserving more explicit attention, 4, 15, 30; dimensions of, 36–37; as educational mechanism, 17–18; education policy and, 38–39; empirical support and, 43; evaluator role in developing, 7–8; facets of, 6–7; fears and anxieties about, 19; formal, explicit rules and, 5, 16; global shifts in view and, 44 fig.; globalized markets and, 44–45; Great Society initiatives and, 5, 34; as guide for evaluation practice, 3–4, 14, 30; HIV/AIDS programs and, 35–36; identifying effective, 107–108; importance of, 17–18, 30, 34–36; informal, implicit rules and, 5–6, 16; inward gaze and, 34, 36, 40; legislative language and, 45; as made in real time, 6; memory and hope in, 43–44, 46–48; meta-evaluation criteria and, 47; methodology and, 6, 19, 42; new world powers and, 45; opportunities and, 28–30; organizational impact and, 37–39; outward view and, 43–44, 44 fig.; power and control and, 18–19; professional associations and, 108; Pushmi-pullyu analogy and, 34, 40; Second Chance Act and, 37; setting of, 7; as shaping evaluation practice, 3–4, 16, 18; sorrowful world possibilities and, 46; stakeholder involvement and, 42; substantive policy and, 15–16; suggestions on developing, 7; taxonomies and, 28, 107–108; theoretical language and, 14; theories and, 17; underlying beliefs about, 3–4; Upward Bound program and, 36. *See also* Brussels, evaluation in; Challenges, for evaluation policy; Dimensions, of evaluation policy; European Union evaluation; Evaluation policy instruments; Model, of evaluation policy; Netherlands, evaluation policy in; Opportunities, for evaluation policy; Political context, of evaluation policy; Principles, of evaluation policy; Taxonomy, of evaluation policies

Evaluation policy instruments: economic, 106; information, 106; regulatory, 105–106; Trochim's evaluation policy wheel model and, 22 fig., 22–24, 105; Vedung's carrot-and-stick analogy and, 105

Evaluation policy wheel, 22 fig., 22–24. *See also* Model, of policy evaluation

Evaluators: globalized markets and, 45; influence of, on policy, 108; morale of, 55–56, 61–63; role of, in developing evaluation policy, 7–8

F
Fetterman, D., 17
Furubo, J.-E., 68, 80

G
Gandhi, A. G., 97
Globalized markets, 44–45
Government, evaluating policy in. *See* Political
    context, of evaluation policies; Political pres-
    sure; U.S. Government Accounting Office
    (GAO), policy evaluation in; *and other U.S.*
    government agencies
Government Performance and Results Act, 105
Great Society, program evaluation in, 5, 34
Grob, G., 8

H
Haas, E. B., 78
Hargraves, M., 28
Hayward, J., 68
Hierarchical organizations, policy in, 26 fig.,
    26–27
HIV/AIDS program evaluation, 35–36, 48
Hjern, B., 68
Hoogerwerf, A., 88
House Select Committee on Congressional Oper-
    ations, 57
Howlett, M., 7

I
Immigration Reform and Control Act (IRCA),
    61–63
Institute for Program Evaluation (IPE), of U.S.
    General Accounting Office, 56–58, 60–61
Institute of Education Sciences, 38
Institute of Medicine, 48
Intent-to-treat (ITT) analyses, 36
International Atlas of Evaluation, 68–69
International evaluation. *See* European Union
    evaluation

J
Judson, H. F., 54
Julnes, G., 18, 40, 103

K
Kaftarian, S. J., 17
Kagan, R., 46
Kane, M., 20
Kennedy, J. F., 15
Kickert, W., 80
King, J. A., 18
Klein Haarhuis, C. M., 94
Klimschot, J., 56
Kordes, F. G., 91
Kulu-Glasgow, I., 95

L
Leeuw, B., 95
Leeuw, F. L., 1, 7, 8, 91, 92, 93, 95, 96, 100, 102

Leviton, L. C., 5
Lindblom, C. E., 75
Lundry Foundation, 48

M
McLean, B., 4
Majone, G., 78
Mark, M. M., 3, 5, 12, 103, 109
Marks, G., 78
Menon, A., 68
Mertens, F., 96
Merton, R. K., 41
Mevissen, J., 95
Ministry of Finance, Republic of Lithuania, 79
Ministry of Public Finance, Romania, 81
Mitrany, D., 78
Model, of evaluation policy: capacity building
    policies and, 20; evaluation policy wheel and,
    22 fig.; goal policy and, 20, 23 fig.; hierarchi-
    cal policy and, 26 fig., 26–27; management
    policies and, 21; meta-evaluation policies and,
    21; principles of, 24 fig., 24–27; process and
    method policies and, 21, 23 fig.; role policies
    and, 21; structure of, 22–24; taxonomy of,
    19–22; use policies and, 21. *See also* Evalua-
    tion policy; Evaluation policy wheel; Princi-
    ples, of evaluation policy; Taxonomy, of
    evaluation policy
Moynihan, D. P., 60
Mulder, H. P., 93
Murphy, R. P., 58
Murphy-Graham, E., 97

N
National Center for Education Evaluation and
    Regional Assistance, 49
National Highway Traffic Safety Administration
    (NHTSA), 58
National Intelligence Council, 44
National Treasury, 5
Netherlands, evaluation policy in: accountability
    and, 89; Budget and Accounts Act and, 89, 91,
    96–97; *Cabinet Memorandum on Policy Evalua-*
    tion and, 93–94; creation of policy appraisals
    and, 97; current budgetary pressures and, 100;
    current day, 98–99; emphasis on methodolog-
    ical criteria and, 97; European Evaluation Soci-
    ety and, 96; European Union pressure and, 97;
    ex post evaluation and, 89–90; future trends,
    99–100; impact of budget deficit on, 90;
    increase in oversight inspectors and organiza-
    tions and, 95–96; influence of Parliament and,
    90–91; lack of information on program impact
    and, 90; methodological quality standards and,
    95; Ministry of Finance and, 88–89, 91;
    national applied research programs and, 89;
    National Audit Office and, 88–89, 91–94, 99;
    New Public Management movement and, 92;
    1980s: birth of evaluation policy, 90–93;
    1990s: formal evaluation policy, 93–96; 1970s
    and before: no evaluation policy, 88–90;
    performance measures and, 95; performance

paradox and, 100; policies on definition, need, and location of evaluation, 93–95; policy type and extent and, 98 fig.; professional evaluation societies and, 96; public criticism and, 100; public input model of government and, 95, 99; reconsideration studies and, 92, 106; reliance on professional communities and, 99; responsive administrative culture and, 92–93; social policy research and, 89; socio-economic background and, 87–88; 2000s: increased formalization and evaluation, 96–97

New Directions for Evaluation: caveats regarding, 10–11; origins in 2008 AEA annual conference and, 9–10; on policies to promote, 40

New Economic Recovery Act, 45

Newcomer, K., 97

Niemeijer, E., 94

O

Obama, B., 15, 30–31

Omnibus Budget Reconciliation Act (OBRA), 60–61

Opportunities, for evaluation policy: audit methodologies and, 28; evaluation working groups and, 28–29; harmonizing, with other policies, 30; policy clearinghouses and archives and, 29, 107; policy consultation and, 29–30; software systems and, 29

Overseas Development Institute (ODI), 49

P

Patton, M. Q., 17

Perry Preschool evaluation, 5

Petrosino, A., 97

Pochet, P., 75

Policy: characteristics of, 15, 17; consciousness and, 17; consequence and, 17; dynamic life of, 15; evaluation vs. substantive, 15–16; guidelines, standards, and theories vs., 17; hierarchical organizations and, 26 fig., 26–27; role of evaluation in, 15–16. *See also* Evaluation policy; Substantive policy

Policy statements: of Barack Obama, 15; characteristics of, 15; clear time-frame and, 15; general nature of, 15; of John F. Kennedy, 15

Policy wheel. *See* Evaluation wheel

Political context, of evaluation policy: agency history and, 64; conflicting loyalties and, 64; constant flux in, 54; defensive tactics and, 64; European Union and, 106; evaluative credibility and, 55, 59–61; evaluative independence and, 54–55, 58–59, 64; evaluative requirements for, 54–56; evaluator morale and, 55–56, 61–63; levels of political pressure and, 52–54; need for current information and, 63–64; recommendations about, 63–65; understanding of bureaucratic mechanisms and, 65. *See also* U.S. Government Accounting Office (GAO), policy evaluation in

Political pressure: bureaucratic climate and, 52–53; cross-branch politics and, 52–53; dominant professional culture and, 52–54, 64; evaluative credibility and, 59–61; evaluative

independence and, 58–59; evaluator morale and, 61–63; levels of, 52–54

Pollitt, C., 68, 78

Porter, D. O., 75

Post, H. M., 89

Preskill, H., 17

Principles, of evaluation policy: accountability and, 24 fig., 25; continuity and, 24 fig., 25; delegation and, 24 fig., 25; encapsulation and, 24 fig., 25; exhaustiveness and, 24 fig., 25; inheritance and, 24 fig., 25; specificity and, 24, 24 fig. *See also* Evaluation policy

Professionals, definition of, 53

Program Assessment Rating Tool (PART), 8, 18, 36

Program Evaluation and Methodology Division (PEMD), of U.S. General Accounting Office, 56, 58, 61, 63

Public Health Service, 106

Public policy, 15. *See also* Substantive policy

R

Raad Maatschapelijke Ontwikkeling (RMO), 100

Randomized controlled trials (RCTs), 6

Reading First program, 42

Regeling prestatiegegevens en evaluatieonderzoek rijksoverheid (RPE), 96, 97

Rist, R. C., 68

Rog, D. J., 18, 40, 103

Rosamond, B., 68, 78

Rosenbaum, D. E., 59

Rossi, P., 17

Rozendal, P. J., 91, 92, 93

S

Sabatier, P. A., 75

San Francisco AIDS Foundation, 35

Sandahl, R., 68

Schlesinger, A. M., Jr., 43

Schrijvershof, C., 97

Schweinhart, L. J., 5

Second Chance Act, 37

Shadish, W. R., 5

Singer, J. W., 56

Sociaal Economische Raad (SER), 89

Society for Research on Educational Effectiveness (SREE), 41, 42

South Africa, program monitoring in, 5

Soydan, H., 97

Stern, E., 1, 67, 79, 86

Substantive policy, 15. *See also* Evaluation policy

Summa, H., 96

T

Tavistock Institute, 76

Taxonomy, of evaluation policy: capacity-building policies and, 20–23, 22 fig., 23 fig.; goals policies and, 20–24, 22 fig., 23 fig.; management policies and, 20–23, 22 fig., 23 fig.; meta-evaluation policies and, 20–21, 22 fig., 23 fig.; participation policies and, 20; policy issues and, 105 fig.; process and methods policies

and, 20–23, 22 fig., 23 fig.; role policies and, 20–23, 22 fig., 23 fig.; utilization policies and, 20–23, 22 fig., 23 fig. *See also* Model, of evaluation policy
Toulemonde, L. J., 96
Trochim, W.M.K., 1, 2, 3, 5–6, 12, 13, 20, 24, 28, 32, 37, 94, 103, 109
Trochim's model of policy evaluation. *See* Model, of policy evaluation

U

Uiters, E., 95
Upward Bound, 36
U.S. Department of Education (DOE), 5, 18, 38–39
U.S. Department of Health and Human Services, 5, 42
U.S. Food and Drug Administration (FDA), 4
U.S. Government Accounting Office (GAO), policy evaluation in: Aid to Families with Dependent Children (AFDC) program and, 59–61; Evaluation and Methodology Division and, 56, 58, 61, 63; evaluative credibility and, 59–61; evaluative independence and, 58–59; evaluator morale and, 61–63; fuel efficiency study and, 58–59; Immigration Reform and Control Act and, 61–63; interagency rivalry and, 57; Institute for Program Evaluation and, 56; political context in, 56; Program Evaluation and Methodology Division and, 56, 58, 61, 63. *See also* Political context, of evaluation policy
U.S. Office of Management and Budget (OMB): AEA Evaluation Policy Task Force and, 8; Program Assessment Rating Tool and, 8, 18
U.S. Senate, 4

USGAO/GGD, 62
USGAO/PEMD, 55

V

van Dam, J.H.A., 91
van der Doelen, F.C.J., 106
van der Knaap, P., 95
van der Mei, W., 92
van Hoesel, P., 95
van Thiel, S., 100
van Vught, F., 80
Vedung, E., 74, 105, 106
Viadero, D., 38
Vioxx, 4
Visser, R. K., 90
von Meyenfeldt, L., 97

W

Walker, W. E., 56
Wandersman, A., 17
Weiss, C. H., 93, 97
White, H., 42, 45
Whitmore, E., 18
Willemsen, F., 95
Wilms, P., 97
Wilson, J. Q., 53
Wollman, H., 68
WRR, 100

Y

Youngs, P., 49

Z

Zakaria, F., 44
Zeitlin, J., 75, 76

NEW DIRECTIONS FOR EVALUATION

ORDER FORM SUBSCRIPTION AND SINGLE ISSUES

DISCOUNTED BACK ISSUES:

Use this form to receive 20% off all back issues of *New Directions for Evaluation*.
All single issues priced at **$23.20** (normally $29.00)

TITLE

ISSUE NO.

ISBN

_____ _____ _____

_____ _____ _____

_____ _____ _____

Call 888-378-2537 or see mailing instructions below. When calling, mention the promotional code JB9ND to receive your discount. For a complete list of issues, please visit www.josseybass.com/go/ev

SUBSCRIPTIONS: (1 YEAR, 4 ISSUES)

☐ New Order   ☐ Renewal

U.S.	☐ Individual: $85	☐ Institutional: $256
CANADA/MEXICO	☐ Individual: $85	☐ Institutional: $296
ALL OTHERS	☐ Individual: $109	☐ Institutional: $330

Call 888-378-2537 or see mailing and pricing instructions below.
Online subscriptions are available at www.interscience.wiley.com

ORDER TOTALS:

Issue / Subscription Amount: $ _____

Shipping Amount: $ _____
(for single issues only – subscription prices include shipping)

Total Amount: $ _____

SHIPPING CHARGES:

First Item $5.00
Each Add'l Item $3.00

(No sales tax for U.S. subscriptions. Canadian residents, add GST for subscription orders. Individual rate subscriptions must be paid by personal check or credit card. Individual rate subscriptions may not be resold as library copies.)

BILLING & SHIPPING INFORMATION:

☐ **PAYMENT ENCLOSED:** *(U.S. check or money order only. All payments must be in U.S. dollars.)*

☐ **CREDIT CARD:**   ☐ VISA   ☐ MC   ☐ AMEX

Card number _____ Exp. Date _____

Card Holder Name _____ Card Issue # _____

Signature _____ Day Phone _____

☐ **BILL ME:** *(U.S. institutional orders only. Purchase order required.)*

Purchase order # _____
Federal Tax ID 13559302 • GST 89102-8052

Name _____

Address _____

Phone _____ E-mail _____

Copy or detach page and send to: **John Wiley & Sons, PTSC, 5th Floor**
989 Market Street, San Francisco, CA 94103-1741

Order Form can also be faxed to: **888-481-2665**

PROMO JB9ND

JB JOSSEY-BASS™

▸ New and Noteworthy Titles in **Research Methods**

Research Essentials: An Introduction to Designs and Practices,
*Stephen D. Lapan (Editor), MaryLynn T. Quartaroli (Editor), ISBN:
9780470181096, Paperback, 384 pages, 2009, $75.00.*

**Research Methods for Everyday Life: Blending Qualitative and
Quantitative Approaches**
*Scott W. VanderStoep, Deidre D. Johnson, ISBN: 9780470343531,
Paperback, 352 pages, 2009. $75.00.*

Methods in Educational Research: From Theory to Practice
*Marguerite G. Lodico, Dean T. Spaulding, Katherine H. Voegtle, ISBN:
9780787979621, Hardcover, 440 pages, April 2006, $75.00.*

SPSS Essentials: Managing and Analyzing Social Sciences Data
John T. Kulas, ISBN: 9780470226179, Paperback, 272 pages, 2008, $45.00.

Quantitative Data Analysis: Doing Social Research to Test Ideas
*Donald J. Treiman, ISBN: 9780470380031, Paperback, 480 pages, 2009.
$75.00*

Mixed Methods in Social Inquiry
*Jennifer C. Greene, ISBN: 9780787983826, Paperback, 232 pages, 2007,
$45.00.*

Action Research Essentials
*Dorothy Valcarel Craig, ISBN: 9780470189290, Paperback, 272 pages, 2009.
$45.00.*

**Designing and Constructing Instruments for Social Research and
Evaluation**
*David Colton, Robert W. Covert, ISBN: 9780787987848, Paperback, 412
pages, 2007, $55.00.*

AEA members: Take advantage of your 20 percent discount on these
titles by ordering at **(877) 762-2974** or www.josseybass.com or and
entering code **AEAF9.**

JB JOSSEY-BASS™

▸ New and Noteworthy Titles in **Evaluation**

**Program Evaluation in Practice: Core Concepts and Examples for
Discussion and Analysis**
*Dean T. Spaulding, ISBN: 9780787986858, Paperback, 176 pages, 2008,
$40.00*

Evaluation Essentials: Methods For Conducting Sound Research
*Beth Osborne Daponte, ISBN: 9780787984397, Paperback, 192 pages, 2008,
$60.00.*

Evaluation Theory, Models, and Applications
*Daniel L. Stufflebeam, Anthony J. Shinkfield, ISBN: 9780787977658,
Hardcover, 768 pages, 2007, $70.00.*

Logic Modeling Methods in Program Evaluation
*Joy A. Frechtling, ISBN: 9780787981969, Paperback, 160 pages, 2007,
$48.00.*

**Evaluator Competencies: Standards for the Practice of Evaluation in
Organizations**
*Darlene F. Russ-Eft, Marcie J. Bober, Ileana de la Teja, Marguerite Foxon,
Tiffany A. Koszalka, ISBN: 9780787995997, Hardcover, 240 pages, 2008,
$50.00*

Youth Participatory Evaluation: Strategies for Engaging Young People
Kim Sabo Flores, ISBN: 9780787983925, Paperback, 208 pages, 2007, $45.00

**Performance Evaluation: Proven Approaches for Improving Program
and Organizational Performance**
*Ingrid J. Guerra-López, ISBN: 9780787988838, Paperback, 320 pages, 2008,
$45.00*

AEA members: Take advantage of your 20 percent discount on these
titles by ordering at **(877) 762-2974** or www.josseybass.com or and
entering code **AEAF9.**